# Trinidad and Tobago

Cavendish Square
New York

Published in 2020 by Cavendish Square Publishing, LLC
243 5th Avenue, Suite 136, New York, NY 10016

Copyright © 2020 by Cavendish Square Publishing, LLC

Third Edition

Library of Congress Cataloging-in-Publication Data

Names: Yong, Jui Lin, author. | Oswald, Vanessa, author. | Sheehan, Sean, 1951- author.
Title: Trinidad and Tobago / Yong Jui Lin, Vanessa Oswald, and Sean Sheehan.
Description: Third edition. | New York, NY : Cavendish Square Publishing, 2020. | Series: Cultures of the world | Includes bibliographical references and index.
Identifiers: LCCN 2019059491 (print) | LCCN 2019059492 (ebook) | ISBN 9781502655813 (library binding) | ISBN 9781502655820 (ebook)
Subjects: LCSH: Trinidad and Tobago--Juvenile literature.
Classification: LCC F2119 .S54 2020  (print) | LCC F2119  (ebook) | DDC 972.983--dc23
LC record available at https://lccn.loc.gov/2019059491
LC ebook record available at https://lccn.loc.gov/2019059492

Editor: Kristen Susienka
Copy Editor: Nathan Heidelberger
Designer: Jessica Nevins

Find us on

# CONTENTS

TRINIDAD AND TOBAGO TODAY **5**

**1. GEOGRAPHY**

Topography • Ecosystems • Forest life • Savanna • Wetlands • Pristine beaches • The coast • Tropical climate • Urban areas **9**

**2. HISTORY**

First peoples • Under Spanish rule • French and British residents • Slavery • Abolition of slavery • Changing hands in Tobago • Petroleum industry • Racism and World War I • World War II • Political parties • After independence **21**

**3. GOVERNMENT**

Road to independence • Divided politics • The judiciary • Crime rate • Political luminaries **35**

**4. ECONOMY**

Oil and gas production • Petrochemical industries • Farming • Cocoa • Developing tourism • Fishing • Recovering from recession **45**

**5. ENVIRONMENT**

Water pollution • Air contamination • Conservation efforts • Recycle and reuse • Water security and waste management • Plants and animals • National parks and protected places **55**

**6. TRINIDADIANS AND TOBAGONIANS**

First inhabitants • European population • African population • Other populations • Hospitality **67**

**7. LIFESTYLE**

Black culture • Indian culture • White culture • City living • City housing • Shopping • Country living • Living in Tobago • Schooling and health care • Getting around • Getting married **73**

**8. RELIGION**

Religious numbers • Christianity • Orisha worship • Shouter Baptists • Rastafari • Hindu worship • The Islamic religion • Superstitions • Obeah **83**

**9. LANGUAGE**

Creole languages • Trinidadian and Tobagonian Creole • French influence • Hindi influence • Spanish influence • Media outlets **93**

**10. ARTS**

Steel bands • Island music • Holiday music • Literary history • Art museums **101**

**11. LEISURE**

The art of doing nothing • The latest calypso • Fetes and concerts • Shops and markets • Spectator sports • Scouting adventures • Park activities **111**

**12. FESTIVALS**

The magic of Carnival • Hosay festival • Diwali festival • Celebrating Eid al-Fitr **119**

**13. FOOD**

Creole cuisine • Indian cuisine • Beverages and desserts • Food insecurity • Seafood **125**

MAP OF TRINIDAD AND TOBAGO **133**

ABOUT THE ECONOMY **135**

ABOUT THE CULTURE **137**

TIMELINE **138**

GLOSSARY **140**

FOR FURTHER INFORMATION **141**

BIBLIOGRAPHY **142**

INDEX **143**

# TRINIDAD AND TOBAGO TODAY

**D**IVERSITY IS A BIG PART OF THE NATION OF TRINIDAD AND Tobago. It's evident in the people who live there, the wildlife, the delectable cuisine, the different styles of music, and so much more. Made up of two main islands—one called Trinidad and the other called Tobago—and several smaller ones, this one country is located at the southernmost tip of the Caribbean islands, lying only a few miles off the coast of South America near the country of Venezuela. Trinidad and Tobago has been attracting settlers for well over 2,000 years, and this has led to a lively and varied population. Residents and visitors alike enjoy the sights in cities such as Port of Spain, San Fernando, and Scarborough, as well as the beautiful beaches, lush rain forests, and rolling hills of the countryside.

## FLAVOR OF THE ISLANDS

People from all different parts of the world—Africa, Asia, Europe, and more—have found their way to this country and combined their own traditions with those of the islands, forming a unique community. Several languages are spoken in Trinidad and Tobago;

Carnival is one of Trinidad and Tobago's most anticipated festivals of the whole year.

however, Trini, or Trinidadian Creole, remains the language most spoken. This particular language takes elements from several others and fuses them together, creating a unique assortment of sounds.

Unlike in other parts of the world, the blending of cultures has not produced conflict, and the people celebrate their sense of togetherness and national identity. Trinidad and Tobago has managed to welcome overseas visitors without selling its soul to tourism and diluting its own cultural identity in the process.

The people of Trinidad and Tobago know how to enjoy life and are blessed with a very hospitable environment that helps make this possible. Their annual Carnival, which originated in the 18th century, is one of the nation's oldest events and is known as the biggest street party in the Caribbean world. Carnival features dancing, singing, music, vibrant costumes, parades, and cultural competitions. Along with this event, the country has a year-round calendar of other cultural festivities. Locals also often throw fetes, which are parties where friends can get together, relax, and let loose.

## FUTURE STRIDES

While Trinidad and Tobago is one of the most prosperous countries in the Caribbean islands, it has experienced its fair share of economic pitfalls. In 2015, it fell into a recession, experiencing significant gross domestic product (GDP) decreases. However, in 2019, it was able to bounce back after gradual GDP growth the year before. The country used to rely on its ample supply of oil to help fuel its economy; however, oil resources have dwindled. Now, the nation makes its largest profits off of natural gas and the petrochemical industry.

Another issue the country faces is food insecurity. There is a limited amount of arable land for growing crops to strengthen the islands' agricultural sector

and provide food for the nation's people. Most food items are imported to the islands at a cheaper price, eliminating an incentive to buy local produce, which is usually sold at a much higher price. This problem means people have less access to safe and nutritious food, which affects the nation's health as a whole.

Even though the government is aware of these obstacles, it has yet to make significant changes to reverse these unfortunate trends. However, with their willpower and innovative minds, the people of Trinidad and Tobago will hopefully be able to work together to remedy these issues in the future and build a better, thriving, and even more successful nation.

**People buy local goods from farmers at a market in Port of Spain in Trinidad and Tobago.**

# GEOGRAPHY

The geography of Trinidad and Tobago varies, with hills, forests, and valleys.

## 1

Trinidad and Tobago is slightly smaller than the US state of Delaware.

TRINIDAD AND TOBAGO ARE TWO relatively small islands off the northern coast of Venezuela in the Caribbean Sea. They are the two southernmost islands of a chain of islands known as the Windward Islands, or the Islands of Barlovento. Aside from Trinidad and Tobago, this chain includes the islands of Grenada, Dominica, Martinique, Saint Lucia, Saint Vincent, and the Grenadines.

These are part of a 2,000-mile-long (3,220-kilometer-long) chain of islands known as the West Indies, which includes Cuba and Jamaica and stretches from the southeastern coast of Florida to the northern coast of Venezuela. The West Indies separate the Caribbean Sea from the Atlantic Ocean and the Gulf of Mexico.

Trinidad is separated from Venezuela by the Gulf of Paria, which extends 100 miles (161 km) east to west and 40 miles (64 km) north to south. The southern tip of Trinidad is approximately 7 miles (11 km) from Venezuela's mainland. The island has a total area of 1,864 square miles (4,828 square km) and is the more industrialized of the two islands. Tobago, lying 19 miles (30 km) northeast of Trinidad, is smaller, having only a total area of 116 square miles (300 sq km).

# TOPOGRAPHY

The islands of Trinidad and Tobago are basically extensions of mainland South America. Trinidad has three ranges of hills running across it from west to east, protecting it from hurricanes, storms, and other extreme weather. The most significant is the Northern Range, part of a range that starts in the Andes Mountains in Venezuela and extends along Venezuela's Paria Peninsula to the islands. The Northern Range has an average height of about 1,500 feet (460 meters), and its highest point is El Cerro del Aripo (Mount Aripo) at 3,084 feet (940 m). El Cerro del Aripo is also the highest point in all of Trinidad and Tobago. The second range of hills, running through the center of Trinidad, is known as the Central Range. It runs from the southwest to the northeast, and its highest point, Mount Tamana (1,009 feet/307 m), is at the eastern end. The Southern Range follows the southern coast of the island and is largely a series of low hills. Those on the east are known as the Trinity Hills. The low-lying land between the ranges tends to be swampy, fed by the many rivers that run off from the hills. In the northwest of the island is the large Caroni Swamp, and in the east is the Nariva Swamp.

In addition to the hundreds of small rivers flowing down its hills, Trinidad has only two major rivers. The Ortoire in the south stretches for 31 miles (50 km) and empties into the Atlantic Ocean on the east coast. The second major

Trinidad and Tobago are two islands with one central government. Each island is unique and full of fascinating people and places.

*Very few asphalt lakes exist in the world. They include La Brea Tar Pits in Los Angeles, California; Lake Guanoco in Venezuela; and Pitch Lake in Trinidad. Unlike the other two, Pitch Lake is still active. It is the largest natural deposit of asphalt in the world, located at La Brea in southwest Trinidad. Asphalt lakes occur when oil oozes up to the surface of the ground and the more volatile elements evaporate, leaving a residue of naturally occurring asphalt.*

Pitch Lake is the largest natural deposit of asphalt in the world.

*Trinidad's Pitch Lake covers about 100 acres (40 hectares), is 250 feet (80 m) deep, and is thought to contain 10 million tons (9 million metric tons) of asphalt, which is replenished continuously. It is possible to walk across the lake. When Sir Walter Raleigh visited Trinidad in the 16th century, he used the asphalt that he found in the lake to caulk his boats and declared it the best he had ever seen. Today, Pitch Lake is a tourist attraction that draws 20,000 visitors annually.*

river is the Caroni in the northwest. It rises in the Northern Range and flows 25 miles (40 km) toward the mangrove swamps along the northwestern coast.

Tobago is a further extension of the Northern Range of Trinidad. It has a central ridge that runs 18 miles (29 km) southwest to northeast. It is called the Main Ridge.

## ECOSYSTEMS

Trinidad and Tobago has abundant plant and animal life, mainly because of the undeveloped nature of the islands and their different ecosystems, which house a variety of habitats. These islands include part of the Andes Mountains,

*Bird of Paradise Island, better known as Little Tobago, is situated about 1.5 miles (2.4 km) off the northeastern coast of Tobago, near a tiny village called Speyside. The island has been designated a wildlife sanctuary. Once it was home to an introduced species of greater birds of paradise, brought to the island in 1909 by Sir William Ingram, who purchased the island that same year. Because of the birds' abundance, it earned the name Bird of Paradise Island. However, in 1963, Hurricane Flora struck the area, wiping out all of the birds of paradise living on the island. No such birds exist now, and the island has been renamed Little Tobago. However, the island continues to be a sanctuary for various bird species. It's currently uninhabited by humans, but over 50 species of birds live there.*

which gives them a diverse landscape for living things to call home. Four ranges of hills, two large rivers and hundreds of small rivers, an extensive coastline, mangrove swamps, and coral reefs provide many habitats for wild creatures.

Trinidad and Tobago shares a lot of the same flora and fauna as South America. The reason for this is that both islands were connected to the South American mainland around 1,500 and 11,000 years ago, respectively.

## FOREST LIFE

Approximately two-fifths of the land in Trinidad and Tobago is forested. The four ranges of hills are densely covered with rain forests. The tallest trees in these rain forests can reach as high as 150 feet (46 m). Orchids and bromeliads grow in the trees, fastened to the branches and taking their nourishment from the air and dying leaves. Lianas wind their way up tree trunks from the ground. The trees of the rain forest tend to flower in the spring, although in the dry season from December to March, an introduced species, the immortelle tree (*Erythrina micropteryx*), covers the forest in orange flowers. In March, another tree bursts into bloom—the poui tree, with striking yellow blossoms. Before it flowers, it loses its leaves, making the blossoms all the more striking.

Over 400 species of birds have been found in Trinidad, and 170 species have been found in Tobago. Most of these birds live in the forest, mainly high up in the canopy, where they feed on the fruit of the trees as it comes into season. In the hills, at least 2,000 feet (610 m) above sea level, there are yellow-legged thrushes, nightingale thrushes, and blue-gray tanagers. At lower levels but less easy to spot is the unusual oilbird (*Steatornis caripensis*), which lives deep in caves and forages for fruit at night. Young oilbirds were once used for both meat and fuel oil, but they are rare now. A large oilbird has a wingspan of 3 feet (1 m). Locally, it's known as the guacharo.

As a nation, Trinidad and Tobago is also home to a variety of animals, including 100 species of mammals, more than 100 species of reptiles, and 35 species of amphibians. Some of these animals include anteaters, nine-banded armadillos, howler monkeys, capuchin monkeys, porcupines, agoutis, raccoons, opossums, snakes, crocodiles, and lizards. There are also about 70 species of bats and a range of toads and frogs. Ocelots are the largest wildcats that live in the forest. These animals often make their way to cultivated land, where farmers shoot them to protect their domestic animals. There are also insects and arachnids on the island, including scorpions, the pink-toed tarantula, hundreds of species of butterflies, and the Amazonian giant centipede (*Scolopendra gigantea*), known as one of the world's largest centipedes.

## SAVANNA

Typical savanna vegetation is found in the Aripo Savannas Scientific Reserve (ASSR), which is the largest remaining natural savanna ecosystem in Trinidad and Tobago. This nature reserve, made up of 4,450 acres (1,800 ha), is located east of Port of Spain in east-central Trinidad. There are more than 450 species living in the ASSR, with 38 of them being restricted species, meaning their survival is dependent on them remaining in their current environment.

There are also palm marsh and marsh forest ecosystems in the ASSR. Palm trees grow at the edges of the high grassland, and sundew flourishes in this inhospitable land because it is able to trap insects to gain nourishment. There are many bird species here—hummingbirds, the savanna hawk, red-bellied macaws, and parrots.

In 2007, the ASSR was labeled an Environmentally Sensitive Area (ESA) under the Environmentally Sensitive Areas Rules. This area is now known as

Tobago is home to the world's oldest protected rain forest. The Tobago Main Ridge Forest Reserve, which was established on April 13, 1776, is recognized by the United Nations Educational, Scientific and Cultural Organization (UNESCO) as a World Heritage site. This forest reserve includes 16 mammal species and 210 bird species.

## WILD POINSETTIA

*The national flower of Trinidad and Tobago is the chaconia (*Warszewiczia coccinea*), otherwise known as the wild poinsettia, or Pride of Trinidad and Tobago. The flower earned its botanical name from Polish-Lithuanian plant collector Joseph Warszewicz. It was given the title "Chaconia" in honor of the last Spanish governor of Trinidad, Don José María Chacón.*

The chaconia flower is the national flower of Trinidad and Tobago.

*Even though this flower is referred to as the wild poinsettia, it is in no way related to the poinsettia (*Euphorbia pulcherrima*). Both plants, however, have bright-red flowers. Trinidad and Tobago's poinsettias bloom on August 31, which is also the nation's Independence Day. Therefore, they are seen as the pride of the country.*

the Aripo Savannas Environmentally Sensitive Area (ASESA). The Forestry Division and Environmental Management Authority (EMA) both manage this area to help protect its endangered inhabitants.

## WETLANDS

Both Trinidad and Tobago have areas of swampland where rivers meander toward the sea, creating large wet areas that are home to many species of plants and animals. The most characteristic plant life in these areas is the mangrove tree. The tree is able to survive in salt marshes because its roots grow from the trunk above the water line and take in air from the atmosphere. The tree produces seeds that germinate while still attached to the trunk, sending roots into the mud before the seedling falls away from the tree. This prevents the seed from being washed out to sea when the high tide sweeps into the swamp.

The Caroni Swamp in northwestern Trinidad is a nature reserve consisting of 12,000 acres (4,850 ha) of lagoon, forest, and marshland. The scarlet ibis (*Eudocimus ruber*), one of Trinidad and Tobago's national birds, lives here in flocks. This bird is featured on the nation's coat of arms and one-dollar bill. (Trinidad and Tobago's other national bird, the cocrico, lives only in Tobago.)

Besides the scarlet ibis, the more than 100 bird species to be found at Caroni include the cormorant, anhinga, and boat-billed heron. In the waters of the swamp are edible fish and other marine life, including huge garrupas, snappers, tree oysters, mussels, and blue crabs. Iguanas, snakes, and manatees can also be found.

**A scarlet ibis settles in Trinidad's Caroni Swamp.**

The Nariva Swamp, located on the eastern coast of Trinidad and inland from Manzanilla Bay, is the largest mangrove freshwater wetland in Trinidad and Tobago. It has an area of about 23 square miles (60 sq km). This swamp has been designated a Wetland of International Importance under the Ramsar Convention and a forest reserve. It contains the Bush Bush Wildlife Sanctuary and has more than 200 species of birds and other animals, such as West Indian manatees, red howler monkeys, and red-bellied macaws. Along with these more peaceful creatures, there are more ferocious residents, such as anacondas and caimans (reptiles related to alligators).

## PRISTINE BEACHES

The nation of Trinidad and Tobago is home to some of the most beautiful beaches with clear blue waters and white sandy shores. In Trinidad, some of the popular beaches include Maracas Bay Beach, Las Cuevas Bay Beach, Blanchisseuse Beach, and Mayaro Beach. Las Cuevas Bay Beach has a snack bar, picnic tables, changing rooms, showers, and lifeguards on duty every day. For those who want to escape the harsh sunlight, there are even small caves to explore. While Blanchisseuse Beach has prime areas for swimming and relaxing, it also has hiking trails through the rain forest and select areas

Maracas Bay Beach is one of the most popular places visited by tourists and residents of Trinidad.

to spot exotic and endangered wildlife such as the leatherback sea turtle.

Some of the go-to beach spots in Tobago include Pigeon Point Beach, Man-O-War Beach, and Englishman's Bay Beach. Pigeon Point Beach caters to families and children. It is protected by the Buccoo Reef, which contains colorful underwater life people can experience while snorkeling. There is also a beach bar and restaurant on the shore, as well as souvenir shops. Englishman's Bay Beach is a mile-long, U-shaped beach with a freshwater stream flowing through it from the Tobago rain forest. It also has coral reefs, which are home to many tropical fish, along with a small restaurant on the bay's shore.

## THE COAST

Tobago has extensive coral reefs that are home to a variety of colorful fish, such as grunts, triggerfish, parrotfish, and butterfly fish. Buccoo, situated in southwestern Tobago, is a protected marine area, although tourism in past years caused much damage to fire and staghorn coral, sea fans, and sea whips on the reef, as well as many other species in the deeper waters. Over time, the ecosystem has recovered and is among the best coral reefs in the world.

Five species of turtle nest on the beaches of the islands. The largest is the leatherback, which can grow to 7 feet (2.1 m) and weigh over 2,000 pounds (900 kilograms), while the smallest is the olive ridley. Other species of turtle include the green turtle, loggerhead turtle, and hawksbill turtle. All of them share a common nesting habit of coming ashore to bury their eggs in the sand. Turtles are protected during the nesting season; however, they are hunted at other times of the year, placing many of them on worldwide endangered species lists.

On the shoreline, there are several very distinctive trees to be found, such as almond trees. This type of tree produces fruit similar to a peach, but it is merely a vessel to house the almond seed and is not edible, like a peach fruit is. After harvesting the almond seed, the fruit is tossed away. There are also mango trees, coconut palms, royal palms, and traveler's palms.

## TROPICAL CLIMATE

Trinidad and Tobago has a tropical climate of high relative humidity and a dry season between January and May and a wet season between June and December. During the wet season, it rains in the late afternoon each day. June is the wettest month, while February is the driest month. The temperatures vary from the coolest to the hottest months, and mean temperatures range from 77 degrees Fahrenheit (25 degrees Celsius) in February to 85°F (29°C) in April. The prevailing northeast trade winds, with a velocity of about 10 to 20 miles (16 to 32 km) per hour, lower the temperature and bring rain to the eastern side of the islands.

Trinidad and Tobago is typically outside the hurricane zone. Hurricanes tend to form between June and September either to the north of the islands or in the eastern Atlantic Ocean near the Cape Verde Islands, but occasionally the country is hit by a hurricane, notably in 1847, 1933, and 1963, when Hurricane Flora killed over 7,000 people in the Caribbean. The birds of paradise on Bird of Paradise Island are also rumored to have been wiped out during that storm. The country has also been hit with several tropical storms that have done significant damage, such as Tropical Storm Alma in 1974 and Tropical Storm Bret in 2017.

## URBAN AREAS

Port of Spain is the capital of Trinidad and Tobago, located on the west coast of Trinidad. The city lies at the bottom of the peninsula that extends to the Bocas del Dragón, or the Dragon's Mouths, the northern passage in the Gulf of Paria between Trinidad and Venezuela. Port of Spain is the third most populated city on the island, with a population of 37,074 according to the country's last census. The city is culturally diverse, highlighting customs of indigenous, Spanish, English, French, African, Indian, Middle Eastern, Chinese, and Portuguese heritages. Port of Spain is also the largest container port of

Just off the coast of Tobago is the world's largest brain coral. These coral colonies have a spherical shape with a grooved surface, resembling the human brain and earning the coral its nickname.

the islands, exporting both agricultural products and manufactured goods. The city is located on a coastal plain with hills to the east, which form the suburbs of the city. The old part of the city is now the business area and also houses government buildings. There are many well-laid-out parks, including the Queen's Park Savannah, near the Emperor Valley Zoo and Royal Botanic Gardens. The Piarco International Airport, home to the Caribbean's largest airline, Caribbean Airlines, is 16 miles (26 km) outside the city at Piarco.

At the other end of the Gulf of Paria is Trinidad's second most populated city, San Fernando, with a reported population of 48,838. This city lies 35 miles (55 km) south of Port of Spain. Like Port of Spain, it is an important shipping center, and it is located on a flat plain with the hills of the Central Range to the east. San Fernando is an administrative center for the south of the island and was once the home of a community of indigenous Caribs. The city, which is known as an administrative and trading hub of Trinidad and Tobago, services the extensive oil fields of the southern part of the island.

Trinidad's most newly developed city is Chaguanas, located halfway between San Fernando and Port of Spain. Some are calling this town "the new capital of Trinidad," as it is the most heavily populated city, with 83,516 people reported in the last census. There are several shopping centers for residents and tourists alike. It has also become a financial center on the island, as it is home to numerous banking headquarters. Chaguanas, like San Fernando, was once home to a group of native Caribs.

The southern end of Trinidad is dominated by heavy industry, with several towns supporting the workers. Point Lisas Industrial Estate is the major industrial center, which includes a steel mill and several other manufacturing plants. Another urban center is Pointe-à-Pierre, which contains the country's largest oil refinery.

The main town and capital of Tobago is Scarborough, which has a deepwater harbor on the Atlantic coast. The town sits on the steep sides of a hill overlooking Scarborough Harbour. It became the capital of the island in 1769, replacing Georgetown farther to the northeast. Scarborough has a population of about 20,000 and is more rural than the towns of Trinidad, with a few attractions. Fort King George is an

18th-century elevated fort named after King George III, which includes a museum of Tobago's history. Most buildings, other than government ones or the few modern ones, are simple one-story structures with tin roofs. To the west of Scarborough is the Arthur Napoleon Raymond Robinson International Airport. The area around it has many tourist-oriented beach resorts and hotels with close access to the reefs at Buccoo.

Farther northeast along the coast is Roxborough, the second-largest settlement in Tobago. On the northern peninsula of the country lies Charlotteville, which is slightly bigger than a village and is isolated by the surrounding hills. The chief occupation there is fishing.

The village of Charlotteville in Tobago is just one of many villages where fishing is a popular industry.

## INTERNET LINKS

**https://www.bbc.com/news/world-latin-america-20072231**
This is the Trinidad and Tobago country profile on the official BBC News website.

**https://www.britannica.com/place/Trinidad-and-Tobago**
This is an overview of Trinidad and Tobago for *Encyclopedia Britannica*, which includes facts about the country's geography, climate, plant and animal life, and more.

**https://www.nationsencyclopedia.com/economies/Americas/Trinidad-and-Tobago.html**
This is a look at Trinidad and Tobago on the Nations Encyclopedia website, which includes information on the country's geography, industry, and economy.

# HISTORY

Trinidad and Tobago are islands full of history.
Here is 18th-century Fort Milford, in Tobago,
whose ruins can still be seen today.

**2**

BEFORE THE ARRIVAL OF Christopher Columbus on Trinidad in 1498, the island was occupied by various indigenous tribes, who had lived in the area since around 300 BCE. The Trinidad and Tobago area is said to be the first area of the Caribbean islands to have acquired human settlers.

Initial native communities left behind stone tools and shell middens—mounds or deposits of shells and other waste. These middens contain man-made waste that is indicative of a previous human settlement. The two main tribes that came from the South American mainland were the Arawaks (also from the Greater Antilles) and the Caribs (also from the Lesser Antilles).

## FIRST PEOPLES

The first inhabitants of the island of Trinidad were the Arawaks, who lived on the southern part of the island. They were a peaceful tribe from the upper regions of the Orinoco Delta in Guyana. The Arawaks were skilled at hunting, fishing, and farming. They grew crops such as potatoes, maize (a type of corn), and cassava, which they used to make bread. This tribe also wove hammocks, made wood carvings and pottery, and smoked tobacco.

The Caribs, a more violent tribe, settled in the northern part of Trinidad. They originally came from the Orinoco rain forests of Venezuela in South America. Their areas of expertise were sailing, trading, raiding

In 1498, Christopher Columbus named the island of Trinidad after the Holy Trinity, while the name Tobago was added later. Tobago was supposedly named after the indigenous word *tabaco*, a pipe used to smoke tobacco leaves.

This is a rock painting made by either the Carib or Arawak people.

villages, and war. They drove many of the Arawaks out of the area.

The islands continued to be developed by these two groups of people for 500 years. It was their descendants whom Christopher Columbus met when he arrived on the island of Trinidad in 1498. When the Spaniards came to colonize the island, the Arawaks were friendly to them. The Spaniards eventually made the Arawaks their slaves. The Caribs, who did not back down without a fight, battled the Spaniards for their land, but they ultimately lost. Many were wiped out along with the Arawaks.

## UNDER SPANISH RULE

The settlements that Columbus stumbled upon were not permanent. People constantly moved to new areas of cultivation when the old areas became infertile. They lived in small village communities. The work was divided, with women doing domestic chores and the farming, while men did the hunting.

The Spanish did not settle in Trinidad for a century or so; however, they raided it often to capture and enslave the island's indigenous inhabitants. The first Spanish settlement was established by Antonio de Berrio in 1592 at Saint Joseph, originally called San José de Oruña, on Trinidad. For two centuries, the Spanish colony survived but with little investment from the Spanish Crown, and the town was regularly attacked by the British, the French, the Dutch, and pirates. In 1687, missionaries arrived and established communities called missions around the island. The main goal of the missions was to convert the indigenous people to Christianity. The missionaries taught as many as they could their beliefs, as well as how to read, write, and farm. In 1699, one mission was attacked by some of the groups it sought to convert. This uprising saw three priests murdered in San Rafael. In response, Spanish soldiers slaughtered hundreds of indigenous people.

Gradually, European settlers arrived and set up tobacco plantations, but these failed. Cocoa plantations were started later and were more successful until 1725, when the entire industry was wiped out by a crop disease. As more settlers came to Trinidad, they also brought diseases such as smallpox with them, which wiped out most of the indigenous population.

# FRENCH AND BRITISH RESIDENTS

By 1777, Port of Spain was an established colony. However, with the other Caribbean islands having more to offer to settlers, it proved difficult to attract Spanish people to Trinidad. As such, the government began to encourage settlers from the other nearby islands to move there, often with their slaves. Any white immigrant who moved was offered generous land and tax incentives for each family member who accompanied them. By 1787, the population of Trinidad had increased to 10,000.

Sir Thomas Picton was appointed governor of Trinidad in 1797.

Trinidad became more French than Spanish as settlers from the other West Indian islands arrived. The French language was used, and the French tradition of Carnival was introduced. People of color or mixed ancestry were also attracted to the island. Some, such as slaves, had no choice in coming to the island, but others chose to live there in hope for a better future.

In the 1790s, slave trading was allowed on the island, and as years went on, it increased. Prior to this, slaves were brought in by their masters but were never bought and sold on the island of Trinidad itself. Cotton and sugar plantations began to thrive as slavery made cultivation possible. Land was also given out to settlers based on how many slaves they brought with them. Trinidad's Spanish governor Don José María Chacón was in charge of overseeing this policy, which was issued in 1794. Chacón had put a lot of effort into developing the colony's economy, and by the end of his tenure in 1797, Trinidad had become one of the wealthiest islands in the West Indies.

Around this time, Great Britain and France were at war, and the fighting often involved Trinidad, which was technically still a Spanish colony. In 1797, Trinidad was invaded by the British under the command of Sir Ralph

*Sir Thomas Picton was a hero to some and a villain to others. He is most known for his service as a lieutenant-general in the British army during the Iberian Peninsular War from 1807 to 1814 and for being the highest-ranking officer killed at the Battle at Waterloo in 1815. However, before these acts, he served as governor of Trinidad and carried out the brutal torture of some of its residents. One of the most remembered cases was the torture of 14-year-old girl Louisa Calderón, who was accused of conspiring to steal from Port of Spain businessman Pedro Ruiz. After she refused to confess to the crime, Picton ordered for her to be tortured.*

*Even after she was tortured, she refused to confess. Her punishment continued, and she was jailed for eight months, forbidden from seeing her family. The case was eventually dropped, and she was freed.*

*Picton was put on trial in London for the torture inflicted upon Calderón. While he was found guilty, he was never sentenced for his crimes. He also claimed that the torture was legal under the Spanish law at the time, even though the island was under British rule.*

Abercromby, and the Spanish surrendered. The Spanish were offered friendly terms of surrender. However, Sir Thomas Picton, an officer of the British army who was appointed governor of the island, treated the residents, particularly anyone he feared might be planning a rebellion, cruelly. Many people of color were imprisoned and tortured. This reign lasted six years until the governor was replaced. In the same year, 1803, Tobago was invaded by the British. Trinidad subsequently became a Crown colony, ruled directly by Britain and administered by senior British army officer Sir Thomas Hislop, who became governor.

## SLAVERY

Trinidad's development had been hindered by the restrictions on slave trading, which had lasted until 1790. By the time of British rule, abolitionists had begun to lobby the British government to restrict the slave trade in Trinidad. Other West Indian islands had already developed slave economies, and the abolitionists wished to stop another slave economy from developing in Trinidad. The other West Indian colonies agreed, because if Trinidad could not develop its sugar and cotton industries, there would be less competition for them. In 1807, the slave trade was forbidden throughout the British Empire, including in Trinidad, although people who were already enslaved were not freed. In 1812, the British issued an order that all slaves in Trinidad should be registered, and no more slaves could be used on the island beyond those registered. The order was ignored, and illegal slave trading continued.

## ABOLITION OF SLAVERY

Slavery was abolished in Trinidad and the rest of the British Empire in 1834. However, most slaves were required to continue working for their former masters as unpaid "apprentices" for a period of several years. This system had been designed by the British government to smooth the transition between slavery and freedom, but it amounted to an extension of slavery and led to much frustration and conflict. The apprentice system was eventually brought to an end in 1838, and full freedom for the enslaved population of Trinidad was achieved.

The repercussions of the injustice of slavery continued in Trinidad for years after abolition. However, Trinidad's former slaves now found themselves in a stronger bargaining position than those in other parts of the Caribbean. They could negotiate for good wages because there had always been a shortage of slaves, unlike in other West Indian colonies where, even after freedom, former slaves still lived in poverty because there were too many of them to bargain for better wages. Some former slaves on Trinidad took up farm work on the plantations, while others moved to the cities and found work. Still others bought a small holding or squatted on unused land. In 1869, the squatters were allowed to buy their plots of land at a cost of 1 pound per 5 acres (2 ha).

Meanwhile, the sugar and cotton plantations were suffering from a shortage of labor. Recruitment was attempted to attract black Americans, the Chinese on Madeira, and liberated slaves from other colonies, but those who came generally found work in the cities or bought their own small holding. In 1845, the British government began to encourage indentured laborers. In exchange for their passage to Trinidad, laborers from India had to work for a landowner for a certain number of years. The arrangement continued until 1917. In that time, 145,000 indentured laborers made their way to work and live in Trinidad. When their period of service ended, many Indians followed the example of the former slaves and also bought plots of land; however, some returned to their native lands. This increase in and change to the population led to modern Trinidad's ethnic mix.

## CHANGING HANDS IN TOBAGO

Tobago had a more difficult time. The island changed hands 31 times among the French, Dutch, English, and Spanish, often suffering badly at each exchange of ruler, before finally being put under British rule through the Treaty of Paris in 1814. A slave economy emerged based on the cultivation of sugar and cotton, and although liberal legislation was passed allowing slaves to own land and providing allowances for their well-being, a slave rebellion was uncovered in 1801, just before it was to take place. If it had been successful, it would have involved slaves from 16 different estates.

Emancipation came to Tobago at the same time as the other colonies. Because Tobago had become more of a slave economy than Trinidad, it suffered more as a result. As in Trinidad, immigration was encouraged, but unlike in Trinidad, the wages were so low that few people could be persuaded to come. In 1847, a hurricane destroyed many plantations, and the falling price of sugar increased Tobago's distress. For a few years, a system where farm workers shared the crops with the landowner seemed to work, but eventually the landowners were making so little money that the scheme fell through. In 1889, Tobago was made a ward of Trinidad, and the two islands were legally one country for the first time.

By 1900, Port of Spain had become a major urban center for Trinidad and Tobago, and a quarter of the population lived there. Huge numbers of disenfranchised urban poor lived beside rich white settlers from France and England. In 1903, there was a riot in Port of Spain over water shortages. Eighteen

people were killed after being shot by police, and the Red House government building was burned down. Although the riots were about water, they were taken to be an indication of political unrest, and Joseph Chamberlain, Britain's secretary of state for the colonies, sanctioned a representative assembly in Trinidad. In 1913, the assembly was installed; however, the first elections were not held until 1925.

The Red House government building in Port of Spain, Trinidad, was burned down in 1903 during the water riots and rebuilt in 1907.

## PETROLEUM INDUSTRY

The world's first well to produce oil was drilled in 1857 at La Brea near Pitch Lake in southern Trinidad, long before the internal combustion engine would provide a sufficient incentive for the drillers. The well was drilled 280 feet (85 m) deep by the American Merrimac Oil Company.

Oil-burning engines became commercially viable in the 1890s, and Trinidad's economy changed forever. When the British navy began to buy diesel-powered ships, British money and engineering skills poured into Trinidad. During the pioneering days of the oil industry, there were many accidents, but by 1929, the technology had been sufficiently developed.

## RACISM AND WORLD WAR I

During World War I, life became very hard for working men in Trinidad, and there were a lot of strikes and political unrest. Many black men wanted to serve in the war alongside the British to defend their country; however, racism was alive and well during this time. The black men who volunteered to fight for Great Britain were not allowed to fight as equals alongside white soldiers, and they were banned from killing Germans. Instead, they were given other jobs in support services, carrying out duties such as laying telephone lines, digging trenches, or driving ambulances. They were kept in segregated units and commanded by white officers.

The West Indian troops were sent to Taranto, Italy, to act as domestic servants to the white troops. Resentment began to build up due to unfair treatment, and several servants rebelled and were imprisoned. After the war, the returning soldiers told stories of racial discrimination, rapidly followed by news of anti-black demonstrations in Great Britain. The victory celebrations in Trinidad were boycotted, and white businessmen began to feel threatened.

Following World War I, Trinidadians faced unfair labor policies and low wages. To combat this, they started the Trinidad Workingmen's Association (TWA), which demanded higher wages and advocated for Trinidad's working class. In 1919, black dockworkers held a strike for better pay. When they were refused, they walked away from their jobs. When non-union labor was brought in, warehouses were smashed. Workers throughout Trinidad joined in the disturbances. British troops intervened, and leading strikers were arrested and imprisoned. Strikes were made illegal, and newspapers and radical publications were banned. The TWA's campaign eventually resulted in some constitutional reform and labor changes, but only on an individual basis, not throughout the entire country of Trinidad and Tobago.

In 1925, activists campaigned to alter the constitution in order to add elected members to the Trinidad and Tobago Legislative Council. Previously, all members had been appointed by the colony's governor. That year, the

This is a photograph of a sugar plantation in the 1930s in Trinidad and Tobago.

activists were successful. Seven members were elected, including trade union representatives. This was the country's first step toward self-government. However, as a worldwide depression began to hit Trinidad, workers grew poorer, and people began to suffer from hunger. Between 1934 and 1937, hunger marches, strikes, and riots took place on sugar plantations and in the oil fields on the island. In 1937, oil workers began a sit-down strike and were chased away by the police. Two oil wells were set on fire. When police tried to arrest the leader, a crowd attacked them, and a policeman was killed. The strikes spread to other oil fields and other industries, and it began to look like a revolution. British warships were sent to Trinidad, and the strikes fizzled out. Some concessions to the workers' demands were made, and the threat of revolution disappeared. However, the unions had grown strong and remained a threat to employers right up to World War II.

## WORLD WAR II

In 1939, when World War II began, men from Trinidad went to fight against the Axis powers (mainly Germany, Italy, and Japan) all over the world for the

## ERIC WILLIAMS

*Eric Williams was one of the most influential political leaders in Trinidad and Tobago. He helped lead the nation to independence in 1962, and that year, he became the nation's first prime minister.*

*In the 1950s, Williams left the faculty at Howard University in Washington, DC, where he taught social and political science, to return to Trinidad. He founded the political party People's National Movement (PNM) in 1955. The party won the 1956 general election and held power for the next 30 years.*

**Dr. Eric Williams served as prime minister of Trinidad and Tobago from 1962 to 1981.**

*Some of the programs Williams supported were meant to end government corruption and provide aid for sugarcane workers. He also pushed for universal, secular, and compulsory education; birth control; and economic and industrial development. Williams served as prime minister up until his death in 1981.*

Allies, which ultimately included France, Great Britain, the United States, and the Soviet Union.

In the summer of 1940, British prime minister Winston Churchill and US president Franklin Roosevelt made a deal for the United States to use part of Trinidad's land as a naval base. This military base brought several jobs to Trinidad. However, Trinidadians were irritated that Britain could offer up their land without their permission. Warships filled the Gulf of Paria and were hunted by German U-boats, or submarines. Things improved for Trinidadians, though. There was high employment, along with better wages and a roaring nightlife that catered to the American troops. While Germany's surrender came in May 1945, the official end to World War II came in September 1945. That same year, Britain's control over Trinidad and Tobago loosened, and constitutional reforms granted any islander over the age of 21 the right to vote.

## POLITICAL PARTIES

After the war, political groups and individuals with different platforms competed for seats in the legislature. The political parties represented different social and ethnic groups. The strongest was the People's National Movement (PNM), formed and led by Dr. Eric Williams. It was dominated by black nationalist intellectuals and had the support of the trade unions, who wanted to take back the oil fields that had been leased to the United States by Great Britain. The next most powerful group was the People's Democratic Party (PDP), founded by Bhadase Maraj. Largely Indian, the PDP was in favor of international capital.

During the 1961 election, white and Indian homes and businesses were looted by PNM supporters. As racial tensions were high, Trinidadians and Tobagonians went to the polls and gave the PNM a large majority of the votes. The following year, Trinidad and Tobago became an independent state in the Commonwealth of Nations, a political and economic organization made up of former British colonies, under the leadership of Williams.

## AFTER INDEPENDENCE

Although the PNM campaigned against foreign capital and supported trade unions when seeking power, it changed its stance once in control, inviting foreign investment and reducing the power of the trade unions. The opposition PDP faded into the background, and the islands became virtually a one-party state. After a series of strikes for better pay, the Industrial Stabilization Act was passed in 1965, making strikes impossible.

Despite rising oil revenues, things did not improve for the black majority in Trinidad. The educational system did improve their quality of training, but there was still a limited amount of jobs for young blacks. With the banning of strikes and no prospect of improvement, a black power movement developed. Workers began to organize strikes in violation of the law. In 1970, there were black power demonstrations in Port of Spain.

Williams died in 1981 while still holding office. The PNM remained in power following the death of Williams, but its 30-year rule ended in 1986 when the National Alliance for Reconstruction (NAR), formed by former People's National Movement members and opposition parties, won the elections in a landslide victory. The NAR was a multiethnic coalition aimed at uniting citizens of both African and Indian descent. Tobago's Arthur Napoleon Raymond (A. N. R.) Robinson, the political leader of the NAR, was named prime minister. He served from 1986 to 1991. Later, he became Trinidad and Tobago's third president. He served from 1997 to 2003.

In July 1990, the Jamaat al Muslimeen, an extremist Black Muslim group with an unresolved grievance against the government over land claims, tried to overthrow the NAR government. Forty-two insurgents from the group held Robinson and most of his cabinet hostage in the Red House for six days. Yasin Abu Bakr, leader of Jamaat al Muslimeen, appeared on television, announcing that the government had been overthrown and that there should be no looting. Despite his request, widespread arson and rioting took place in Port of Spain, resulting in the deaths of 24 people. After a long standoff

Dr. Keith Christopher Rowley became prime minister of Trinidad and Tobago in 2015.

with the police and military, Yasin Abu Bakr and his followers surrendered to Trinidadian authorities.

In recent years, political control of Trinidad and Tobago has alternated between the PNM and another political party, the United National Congress (UNC). Dr. Keith Christopher Rowley of the PNM was sworn in as prime minister on September 9, 2015, after the PNM won 23 of the 41 seats in the House of Representatives. Rowley had been the leader of the PNM since May 2010.

## INTERNET LINKS

**https://www.britannica.com/place/Trinidad-and-Tobago/History#ref516228**
This is the history section of the Trinidad and Tobago overview from the *Encyclopedia Britannica*.

**https://www.mytobago.info/history.php**
This website gives a brief summary of the history of Tobago.

**https://thecommonwealth.org/our-member-countries/trinidad-and-tobago/history**
This website provides information on the origins and history of Trinidad and Tobago.

**https://www.worldatlas.com/articles/top-10-interesting-facts-about-trinidad-and-tobago.html**
This website provides 10 interesting facts about Trinidad and Tobago.

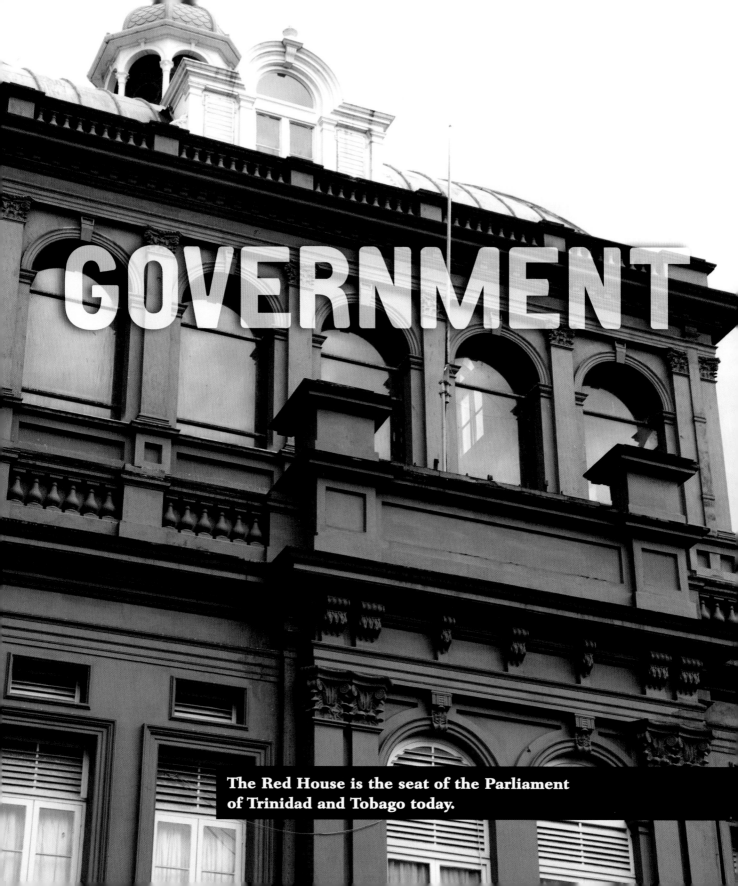

# GOVERNMENT

The Red House is the seat of the Parliament
of Trinidad and Tobago today.

**3**

TRINIDAD AND TOBAGO'S government has gone through several changes over the years. This may be the result of the nation first acquiring a common government in 1889. Prior to that, Tobago was a British colony that was not related to its larger neighbor. Today, the government has diversified and progressed into a mostly stable republic that works to better its people and its country.

## ROAD TO INDEPENDENCE

After the conjoining of the two countries into one nation, the government of Tobago shifted to Trinidad, although Tobago retained separate taxes and a smaller subordinate legislature.

In 1925, the national legislature was reformed, and members were added. This was followed by the achievement of universal suffrage, or the right for everyone (above a certain age) to vote, in 1945. Government rule was carried out by a party-based cabinet, but authority was based in Great Britain.

Trinidad and Tobago's independence came in 1962; however, some links to Great Britain remained. For example, the new nation agreed to follow the British model of government and traditions of a parliamentary democracy. The islands also became part of the British Commonwealth

"We have many highly successful women in our country, but the system itself militates against women rising. Too often, women give up and don't pursue their dreams. I would like to see more women get involved in politics at the highest levels, so that the country would see us for what we are and not pay attention to the shoes we wear and the dress we choose"
—Kamla Persad-Bissessar, first female prime minister of Trinidad and Tobago

and were to be ruled by a governor-general who was not elected by the people but appointed by Britain. The governor had a cabinet made up of elected representatives. Beneath the cabinet was a bicameral, or two-house, legislature, along the lines of the American system today. Both the houses were elected.

In 1976, the current constitution was adopted, and Trinidad and Tobago became a republic headed by a non-executive president, who replaced the governor-general. The sixth and current president is Paula-Mae Weekes. She took office in March 2018. She was elected by an electoral college of all the country's ministers. Below the president is a cabinet chosen by and headed by the prime minister. The prime minister and cabinet are responsible to the legislature, or Parliament.

Parliament consists of two houses. One of them is the House of Representatives, which has 42 members. Of these, 41 are directly elected. The other is the house speaker, who is designated from outside Parliament. Legislation originates and passes from this house to the Senate, which is made up of 31 members. Sixteen senators are appointed by the ruling party, 9 by the president, and 6 by the opposition party. Both representatives and senators serve five-year terms.

Tobago has its own devolved House of Assembly, set up in 1980, which can legislate on some financial matters and other local issues such as urban and rural development, education, health, and housing. It has 16 members—12 of them are elected by a majority vote, and 4 are selected by the leaders of the majority and minority parties. Each member serves for 4 years.

In the most recent elections in Tobago, held in 2017, the PNM won 10 seats, while the Progressive Democratic Patriots won 2 seats.

## DIVIDED POLITICS

For several years after independence, Trinidad and Tobago had a chaotic electoral system with individuals competing for seats in Parliament. Eventually, a series of political parties formed, mostly along racial lines.

The first parties to form before independence were the PNM and PDP; both were formed in the 1950s. The PNM contested the elections of 1956 along with seven other parties. It represented the black middle classes, stood for

*The three colors included in Trinidad and Tobago's national flag are white, black, and red. Each color symbolizes a different aspect of the nation's history, character, and values.*

*Red symbolizes the temperament of the country, its vitality, warmth, and courage. Black represents strength, unity, and the wealth of the country in its oil reserves. White represents purity and equality. The three colors also represent earth (black), water (white), and fire (red)—the three basic elements of life.*

*The majority of the flag is red, with three diagonal bands running from the top left corner to the bottom right corner. These bands consist of one large black band in the middle and two thinner white bands to the left and right.*

*The national flag of Trinidad and Tobago was adopted in 1962 when the nation gained its independence from the British Empire.*

nationalism and better education, and strongly criticized the privileged white elite. The PNM won majorities in most elections from 1956 until 1986, and so the government of Trinidad was in the hands of a party that represented black middle-class interests.

The PDP consisted of mainly Indian people and for many years formed the chief opposition party. In the 1970s, the PDP merged with a radical group, the Action Committee of Dedicated Citizens (ACDC), and became the Democratic Liberation Party (DLP).

In Tobago, the PNM was less influential, and a series of coalitions led by the politician A. N. R. Robinson took control of the assembly. In 1986, the PNM lost power in Trinidad as a coalition of very diverse parties representing big business, trade unions, rural Indians, and all Tobagonians called the National Alliance for Reconstruction (NAR) took power. For the first time, a multiethnic party led the country, but it did not last. In 1991, the NAR collapsed and the PNM returned to power, with Patrick Manning appointed prime minister. He served until 1995.

The 1995 election saw the emergence of another single-race party, the United National Congress (UNC), which was supported mainly by those of Indian descent. Seats in the House of Representatives were split exactly between the two parties, the PNM and the UNC, with two NAR members supporting the UNC. For the first time in Trinidad's history, there was an Indian prime minister, Basdeo Panday. He served until 2001.

A deadlock arose in the House of Representatives in 2001, and President A. N. R. Robinson appointed Manning as prime minister again. This time, he served until 2010. In his final years in office, Manning's popularity dwindled as he was caught in a series of scandals.

In the 2010 election, Kamla Persad-Bissessar, who represented the People's Partnership, a coalition of the UNC and four other parties, defeated the PNM. The People's Partnership won 29 of the 41 seats in the House of Representatives. She became the first female prime minister of Trinidad and Tobago, serving until 2015.

In the 2015 election, Keith Christopher Rowley of the PNM won 23 of the 41 seats in the House of Representatives. He became the eighth prime minister of the Republic of Trinidad and Tobago. Rowley was sworn into office on September 9, 2015.

Today, the main political parties in Trinidad and Tobago include the PNM and the various parties that make up the People's Partnership, including the UNC, the Congress of the People (COP), the Tobago Organization of the People, and the National Joint Action Committee.

**Patrick Manning first became prime minister of Trinidad and Tobago in 1991. He returned to office in 2001.**

## THE JUDICIARY

Trinidad and Tobago's judicial system is a branch of the government that interprets and applies the laws of the country to ensure equal justice under the law and to provide an outlet for legal disputes. It is based on the British legal system. The highest court is the Supreme Court of Judicature, which consists of a High Court and a Court of Appeal, and has establishments in Port of Spain, San Fernando, and Tobago. The chief justice of the Supreme Court, otherwise known as the head of the judiciary, is appointed by the president,

*Kamla Persad-Bissessar and Paula-Mae Weekes both have made history as two of Trinidad and Tobago's most influential female political leaders.*

*Persad-Bissessar was born in Siparia, a rural community in southern Trinidad, on April 22, 1952. As a young girl, she was interested in technology and reading novels. After graduating from Iere High School, she went on to further her education at various universities. She has received many diplomas and certificates at the undergraduate and graduate levels in the subjects of education, law and legal education, and business. After completing her studies, she worked as a teacher, social worker, lecturer, and attorney-at-law. In 1987, she finally entered politics, becoming an alderman for the Saint Patrick County Council. In 1995, she became a member of Parliament for Siparia. In April 2006, she made history as the first woman to be appointed leader of the opposition in the Republic of Trinidad and Tobago. In 2010, she was elected political leader of the United National Congress and appointed leader of the opposition a second time. Then, in May 2010, she made history again by becoming the first female prime minister of the Republic of Trinidad and Tobago. She served until September 2015.*

**Kamla Persad-Bissessar became the first female prime minister of Trinidad and Tobago in 2010 and served until 2015.**

*Paula-Mae Weekes was born in Port of Spain on December 23, 1958. After attending Bishop Anstey High School, she went on to acquire her bachelor of laws degree at the University of the West Indies, Cave Hill, in 1980 and a legal education certificate from the Hugh Wooding Law School in 1982. Next, she worked in the Office of the Director of Public Prosecutions for 11 years before opening up her own private law practice in 1993. She was appointed as a judge for the criminal division of Trinidad's High Court in 1996 and then judge on the nation's Court of Appeal in 2005, where she served until her retirement in 2016. She went on to join the appellate branch of the Judiciary of the Turks and Caicos until 2018. After this, she campaigned as a presidential candidate for the PNM government of Prime Minister Keith Rowley. On March 19, 2018, she took office as the first woman to hold the post of president of Trinidad and Tobago and the nation's second female head of state, after Queen Elizabeth II.*

on the advice of the prime minister and the leader of the opposition. In all, there are 35 judges at the High Court level and 11 for the Court of Appeal.

Currently, the final court of appeal for Trinidadians is the Privy Council in London, England. However, Trinidad and Tobago was part of the creation of the Caribbean Court of Justice (CCJ), which was inaugurated on April 16, 2005, and is based in Port of Spain. The CCJ was created to replace the Privy Council as the final court of appeal for the member states of the Caribbean Community (CARICOM), which includes 20 countries—15 that are full members and 5 that are associate members. Full members include Antigua and Barbuda; Barbados; Belize; Dominica; Grenada; Guyana; Jamaica; Saint Kitts and Nevis; Saint Lucia; Saint Vincent and the Grenadines; Suriname; and Trinidad and Tobago. While all states were expected to become full signatories of the CCJ, only Barbados, Belize, Dominica, and Guyana have agreed to the authority of the CCJ. All the other CARICOM countries, including Trinidad and Tobago, have been taking steps toward making the CCJ their final court of appeal.

Below the higher courts, there is the Magistracy, which is a system of magistrate courts to deal with less important matters.

All primary posts in the judicial system are filled at the discretion of the president and prime minister. Judges can serve until the age of 65, at which point they must retire.

## CRIME RATE

Currently, the government of Trinidad and Tobago is facing several challenges when it comes to reducing crime in the country, according to the Trinidad and Tobago 2019 Crime and Safety Report. The country faces an ongoing battle against drug trafficking and gang-related violence, which has created a problem of imported illegal weapons, including firearms. The Trinidad and Tobago Police Service (TTPS) 2018 crime statistics recorded that 80 percent of murders carried out in the country involved firearms.

The murder rate has increased every year since 2014, according to the TTPS statistics. In 2018, there were 517 murders nationwide, an increase by more than 100 deaths since the 403 murders reported in 2014. The murder rate continues to be driven by gang- and drug-related activity. The majority

*In 1996, a gang of nine men murdered a family in Williamsville, Trinidad. After being found guilty of the murder, the nine men were sentenced to death, a mandatory punishment for murder under Trinidad and Tobago law. The men's lawyers took their case to the Privy Council in London in May 1999, but more than the lives of these nine men was resting on the Privy Council's decision.*

*Tension was high among the Caribbean countries, many of which also use the British Privy Council as a last court of appeal, since the sovereign rights of Trinidad and Tobago would be challenged if the Privy Council commuted the sentence. The Privy Council upheld the conviction, and the nine men were executed in June 1999, despite pleas for mercy by Archbishop Desmond Tutu and other international figures. The nine men were all drug racketeers, and 80 percent of public opinion in Trinidad supported the death penalty.*

*While this decision of the Privy Council should have ensured that men on death row all over the Caribbean would now face the death penalty, none have been executed since these nine men. The reason for this is the 1993 landmark case of* Pratt and Morgan v. the Attorney General of Jamaica, *in which it was decided that the death penalty should be implemented within five years of conviction, otherwise it is considered inhumane punishment. This has resulted in many prisoners having their death sentences reduced to life imprisonment.*

*Many people in Trinidad and Tobago believe the death penalty should be enforced to deter people from committing crimes in the country. However, there are also a number of people who think the Privy Council in London should not have the authority to decide on the death penalty of those in the Caribbean.*

of the murders that happen within Trinidad and Tobago occur on Trinidad. There were only 9 murders on Tobago in 2018.

About one-third of all crimes in Trinidad and Tobago result in arrest.

## POLITICAL LUMINARIES

While many Trinidadians agree that the most important political figure and charismatic leader in Trinidad and Tobago was Eric Williams, there are many

## TERRORISM THREATS

*Despite the fact that there have been few terrorist threats within Trinidad and Tobago over the last five years, it remains an issue for the country in the 21st century. According to the Trinidad and Tobago 2019 Crime and Safety Report, there is a moderate risk of terrorism in Port of Spain. There are several extremist and terrorist groups operating in the country; however, most of these groups have not carried out any of their supposed plans.*

*Several incidents in 2015 pointed to terrorist activity, such as a Trinidadian being accused of studying terrorist tactics in Saudi Arabia. He was put in a Saudi prison for 16 months and released and returned to Trinidad and Tobago in 2016. Since 2014, there have been various videos featuring several young men who claim to be Trinidadian nationals declaring their support for ISIS, a terrorist group centered in the Middle East.*

*In 2015, Trinidadian national Kareem Ibrahim was deemed a terrorist by the Trinidad and Tobago High Court. The state proceeded to freeze his local assets in accordance with the Anti-Terrorism Act of 2005, which lays out strict laws for people accused of such crimes. This judgment set a legal example for future terrorism rulings.*

*In 2017, the US government deemed Trinidadian ISIS fighter Shane Crawford, also known as Abu Saad al-Trinidadi, a terrorist.*

*Since the border control is weak in Trinidad and Tobago, there is a continued concern that terrorists will use the country as a place to carry out terrorist activity.*

other important people who have played a part in Trinidad and Tobago's political life.

Bhadase Maraj was the president of the Sanatan Dharma Maha Sabha, an orthodox Hindu association. He took an active part in politics, as he founded and led the People's Democratic Party (PDP), which later evolved into other parties. He represented the Indian equivalent of what Williams stood for, but he was never able to mobilize Indian Muslims to his side. He was succeeded as party leader in 1960 by Rudranath Capildeo, an Indo-Trinidadian from an academic background.

Another memorable political leader in Trinidad and Tobago was Basdeo Panday, who was a young lawyer in 1971 when he became interested in politics and was persuaded to lead a party called the United Labour Front (ULF), which became the leading opposition party of the mid-1970s. A. N. R. Robinson became an ally of Panday's in the 1980s when they formed the National Alliance for Reconstruction. That act ultimately helped Robinson win the election for prime minister. Panday followed Robinson in 1995, becoming Trinidad and Tobago's first Indian prime minister. Even after his time in office ceased, he took an active part in the country's politics for many years.

In the 21st century, Trinidad and Tobago has also welcomed more female politicians, such as Kamla Persad-Bissessar, who has pushed to promote gender equality and urged more women to participate in politics. Since leaving her post as prime minister and serving as leader of the UNC, she has also expressed the need for a domestic violence fund and a special police force unit to help victims of abuse.

Bhadase Maraj (*speaking*) founded the People's Democratic Party in Trinidad and Tobago.

## INTERNET LINKS

**https://caricom.org/about-caricom/who-we-are**
This website provides information on CARICOM and how it functions to benefit Trinidad and Tobago's economy.

**http://nathulaw.com/understanding-the-court-system-in-trinidad -and-tobago**
This article helps to explain Trinidad and Tobago's court system.

**https://thecommonwealth.org/our-member-countries/trinidad -and-tobago/constitution-politics**
This website includes information on Trinidad and Tobago's government and political history.

# ECONOMY

For many years, oil was the main industry in Trinidad and Tobago. It still remains important today.

**4**

TRINIDAD AND TOBAGO IS ONE OF the richest countries in the Caribbean and also has one of the highest gross domestic products per capita in the Western Hemisphere. It has a mixed economy, with some areas being owned and run by the state, while the majority are run by private enterprise.

Trinidad and Tobago has earned a reputation as an excellent investment site for international businesses, and it had one of the highest growth rates in the region in the early 2000s. Its economy's growth is fueled by investments in liquefied natural gas (LNG) and petrochemicals, which are chemicals taken from petroleum and natural gas. The country has been able to profit off of these resources for years due to its large oil and natural gas reserves. However, these reserves, especially the oil reserves, are beginning to dwindle. The country is also a regional financial center, and tourism has become a steadily growing industry, although it is not proportionately as important as in many other Caribbean nations. Apart from oil and gas production, another major industry is manufacturing. This sector includes sugar processing, car assembly, radio and television production, paper products and printing, cement, furniture, processed foods, and clothing.

The economy is challenged by factors such as low labor productivity, government bureaucracy, and corruption, which have affected growth in the 21st century. The currency is the Trinidad and Tobago dollar. As of early 2020, 1 US dollar equaled 6.76 in Trinidad and Tobago dollars.

## CARICOM SINGLE MARKET AND ECONOMY

*In the late 1980s, CARICOM members agreed to establish the CARICOM Single Market and Economy (CSME), encompassing Trinidad and Tobago and several other Caribbean countries, including Antigua and Barbuda, Barbados, Belize, Dominica, Grenada, Guyana, Jamaica, Saint Kitts and Nevis, Saint Lucia, Saint Vincent and the Grenadines, and Suriname. The CSME allows for the free movement of goods, services, persons, capital, and technology between all of these countries. It also gives permission to any business owner in the CSME to establish a business in any of the participating countries.*

*The CSME has affected industries within Trinidad and Tobago, such as the fishing industry. For example, in April 2006, the Permanent Court of Arbitration issued a decision that set up a maritime boundary between Trinidad and Tobago and Barbados and compelled Barbados to enter a fishing agreement that limited Barbadian fishermen's catches of flying fish in Trinidad and Tobago's exclusive economic zone. With the implementation of the CSME, however, that agreement expired, and now people of both countries are encouraged to fish wherever they want in order for both countries to benefit.*

## OIL AND GAS PRODUCTION

Oil was discovered in Trinidad in 1857 when the world's first well that produced oil was drilled at La Brea. The first oil refinery was built in Trinidad and Tobago at Pointe-à-Pierre between 1916 and 1917. By 1946, Trinidadian oil represented 65 percent of the British Empire's oil production. For many years after, oil dominated the country's economy; however, changes occurred in the early 1990s, when the country's hydrocarbon sector converted from an oil-based one to a mostly natural gas—based one. This negated the need for oil, in favor of the other fossil fuel, natural gas.

Today, Trinidad and Tobago produces almost nine times more natural gas than crude oil, and in the 21st century, the oil industry is being challenged more than ever. In 2018, Prime Minister Keith Rowley ordered Petrotrin, Trinidad's major oil company, to close due to its declining production, lack of profit, and increased debt. The company, which had been in operation for over 100 years, closed after suffering $8 billion in losses over a five-year period. Other oil

Although the economy in Trinidad and Tobago has experienced a boost, at least 20 percent of the population is living in poverty.

companies, such as Heritage Petroleum and Paria Fuel Trading Company, still exist in Trinidad and Tobago. While approximately 1,800 people from Petrotrin lost their jobs, some of them were rehired at other oil companies in the region.

Reserves of crude oil remained steady at 728 million barrels from 2009 to 2016; however, in 2017, they decreased to about 242 million barrels. In March 2019, oil production hit a record low of 51,000 barrels produced a day.

Trinidad and Tobago's Atlantic LNG Company in Point Fortin is one of the largest natural gas liquefaction facilities in the Western Hemisphere. In 2013, natural gas reserves were 25.24 trillion cubic feet (715 billion cubic meters) but declined to 10.6 trillion cubic feet (300 billion cubic m) in 2017. In 2018, however, natural gas production increased by 32.4 percent.

The first oil well in the country was drilled at La Brea. This area is also known for its asphalt, which workers are shown here shoveling around 1890.

## PETROCHEMICAL INDUSTRIES

Several industries have emerged as a result of the development of the oil industry. One example is the petrochemical industry. Petrochemical companies produce by-products of oil for various uses. These by-products include chemicals such as ammonia and methanol. Ammonia can be used to make different kinds of fertilizer. Methanol can be used as a solvent in the production of various chemicals. In 2013, Trinidad and Tobago was the world's largest exporter of ammonia and second-largest exporter of methanol, according to IHS Global Insight.

Trinidad and Tobago's currency, the dollar, is very colorful.

Currently, Trinidad and Tobago has 11 ammonia plants in operation, including two ammonia complexes on the Point Lisas Industrial Estate. The first plant, Yara Trinidad Limited, was opened in 1959, and the most recent one, AUM Ammonia, was opened in 2009. In total, these plants produce 5.7 million tons (5.2 million metric tons) a year.

The production of methanol in Trinidad and Tobago goes back to 1984, when the government opened its first plant, Trinidad and Tobago Methanol Company (TTMC), at Point Lisas Industrial Estate in Trinidad. Since then, the country's methanol industry has expanded with six other plants. Together, these plants produce over 7.3 million tons (6.6 million metric tons) of methanol annually. Methanol Holdings (Trinidad) Limited (MHTL) was once the largest supplier of methanol to North America and continues to be one of the leading suppliers today.

## FARMING

From being a major producer of coffee, sugar, rubber, and cocoa in the 20th century, Trinidad and Tobago has developed a more industrialized economy in the 21st century. Agriculture now accounts for about 0.4 percent of GDP and employs 3.1 percent of the working population. As of 2016, the amount of arable land was at 4.9 percent, and 4.3 percent of the land was used for permanent crops.

*The United States is Trinidad and Tobago's largest trading partner, with over 34 percent of exports going to the United States and nearly 24 percent of imports coming from the United States. In 2018, Trinidad and Tobago exported more than $3.7 billion of goods to the United States and imported $2.1 billion of goods from them. Trinidad and Tobago's leading exports to the United States are liquefied natural gas, methanol, chemicals, and fertilizers. The top products imported from the United States to Trinidad and Tobago include food products, chemical products, and machinery.*

There are two types of agricultural operations. One takes place on a large estate or plantation that is managed by a specialist who hires several laborers. The other is the small farm cultivated by its owner. The large estates mainly focus on commercial export crops, such as citrus fruits, tomatoes, cocoa, sugar, coffee, and cut flowers. The small farms generally produce crops such as corn, rice, peas, beans, potatoes, exotic fruits, and vegetable varieties for the home market; however, they also grow some export crops. Lowland rice is grown almost entirely by Indian farmers. The value of crops grown for the domestic market is believed to be considerably greater than that of the export crops.

The islands have cattle, pigs, and sheep, all owned by small farmers for sale in local markets. Chickens are also an important staple, and water buffalo are kept mainly for transportation and for plowing fields.

## COCOA

The major export crop, cocoa (also called cacao), is produced in the hill sections of both Trinidad and Tobago. Estates produce considerably more cocoa than small farms due to better agricultural practices and because small farmers intercrop bananas, coffee, and other crops with cocoa. The amount of cocoa beans produced per year has decreased significantly over the decades. A century ago, cocoa plants in this country produced 30,000 tons (27,215 metric tons) of cocoa beans per year. As of 2017, only 500 tons (454 metric tons) were being produced annually.

*Ecotourism is a developing industry in Trinidad and Tobago. It involves people traveling to exotic, often threatened, natural environments to take part in activities to support conservation and promote sustainability. Some of these activities include visiting national parks, hiking on nature trails, and educational ecology tours. There are also several tours where tourists can observe wildlife.*

**Leatherback turtles can be found on the beaches of Trinidad and Tobago.**

*One of the most popular ecotourism opportunities on the northern beaches of Trinidad is viewing the nesting areas of leatherback turtles, where thousands of eggs are laid annually. There are also several places for watching a variety of birds, such as toucans, woodpeckers, falcons, and the scarlet ibis, one of Trinidad and Tobago's national birds.*

*A recommended favorite place for ecotourism is Trinidad's Northern Range, in particular the area of Mount Tamana, where there are excellent places to see breathtaking views. This area's main attractions, however, are its bat caves, with 11 species of bats. Between 5:30 p.m. and 7 p.m. every day, visitors can see the 1.5 million bats leave their caves to search the skies for insects or other creatures to eat. Tourists also encounter frogs and snakes while touring these caves.*

*Other spots known for ecotourism are the swamps of Trinidad, such as the Caroni Swamp and the Nariva Swamp. There, tourists can hike through the swamps, search for waterfalls, and observe wildlife such as red howler monkeys, capuchin monkeys, West Indian manatees, and tree porcupines.*

While hurricanes do not typically hit Trinidad and Tobago, they do skirt the islands and bring along weather systems that affect the country's climate and its cocoa yields. The changing weather patterns caused by global warming lead to lower crop yields.

## DEVELOPING TOURISM

Tourism is a growing sector in Trinidad and Tobago. Port of Spain, Trinidad's capital, is a major tourist destination, and most cruise ships enter the islands at Port of Spain Harbor. Scarborough, Tobago's capital, is another destination for tourist ships.

Workers are shown here gathering cocoa beans on a plantation in Trinidad during the early 20th century.

Tourism is centered on Tobago, with most of the beach resorts and tourist hotels concentrated there. It is served by the A. N. R. Robinson International Airport, which is 6.8 miles (11 km) away from Scarborough. This airport has connections to several international hubs.

In 2013, plans were put in place to develop an aerotropolis called Piarco AeroPark near the Piarco International Airport, which is 15.5 miles (25 km) from Port of Spain. An aerotropolis is an urban area centered around an airport. Piarco AeroPark, once built, will feature shopping plazas, retail outlets, a hotel, conference centers, car rental facilities, a service station, a park, and more. It is hoped the new aerotropolis will boost trade and tourism as a whole for Trinidad and Tobago.

## FISHING

The waters of Trinidad and Tobago have always had rich and diverse marine fisheries. However, the challenge today is keeping marine resources, such as finfish, shrimp, lobster, crab, and shellfish, from being exploited. The main legislation in place for fishing is the Fisheries Act of 1916. Though amendments

have been made to this act since then, it is nonetheless out of date. This lack of modern regulation in the fishing industry means there is open access to the waters, which has led to overfishing and overcapitalization.

Although Trinidad and Tobago is a member of several fishing agreements, such as the Convention on International Trade in Endangered Species of Wild Fauna and Flora, the United Nations Fish Stocks Agreement, and the Food and Agriculture Organization Code of Conduct for Responsible Fisheries, a main concern is illegal fishing and lack of policing of such activities. This inattention led to the country receiving a "yellow card," or warning, in 2016 from the European Union.

## RECOVERING FROM RECESSION

Even though Trinidad and Tobago is known for having a strong and successful economy, in 2015 it suffered from four consecutive quarters of negative GDP movement. This was largely due to a decline in the energy sector. The petroleum industry contributed 40 percent to the GDP between 2006 and 2014. However, this industry then took a plunge, only contributing 22 percent to the GDP in 2015 and 2016 after a sizeable drop in international oil prices. This caused the local central bank to announce in December 2015 that the country was entering a recession.

Luckily, Trinidad and Tobago officially recovered from the recession in 2019 after small GDP growth in 2018. The manufacturing industry was one of the leading contributors to economic growth that year, contributing over $32 billion to the country's GDP. Other non-energy sectors that contributed to growth were retail sales and new car registrations from the end of 2018 to early 2019.

While Trinidad and Tobago has relied on the revenue from the oil industry for years, oil reserves are limited in the 21st century, which means the nation needs to focus its attention on areas such as natural gas and agriculture in order to promote GDP growth and generate employment.

In 2019, the unemployment rate in Trinidad and Tobago was 2.8 percent, which is a significant decrease from the 1990s, when it had reached 17.2 percent.

## INTERNET LINKS

**https://www.forbes.com/places/trinidad-and-tobago**
As part of the *Forbes* site, this article gives a brief description of Trinidad and Tobago's economy.

**https://www.heritage.org/index/country/trinidadtobago**
This website gives a background of Trinidad and Tobago's economy.

**https://oec.world/en/profile/country/tto**
This website provides specific data regarding Trinidad and Tobago's economy.

**https://www.worldbank.org/en/country/caribbean/overview**
This website gives overviews of economic situations of various Caribbean countries, including Trinidad and Tobago.

# ENVIRONMENT

Birds like this native Trinidad motmot are just some of the animals seen in Trinidad and Tobago.

## 5

WHILE CHALLENGES STILL LOOM, today Trinidad and Tobago has made environmental conservation more of a significant priority. For years, the country, along with the rest of the world, has experienced the environmental effects of climate change, which has started to directly affect its economy as well. High population density and the industrialized economy have contributed to climate change and threatened Trinidad and Tobago's biodiversity. Environmental issues include water pollution from agricultural chemicals, industrial wastes, and raw sewage; air pollution; deforestation; and soil erosion. This has caused citizens to band together to create and promote sustainable solutions and make Trinidad and Tobago a more environmentally conscious country.

"Through the theme, *Environmental Pride is National Pride,* we urge citizens to care for our nation's environment, preserving its beauty and health for the wellbeing of all our people."
—Ministry of Planning and Development of Trinidad and Tobago

## WATER POLLUTION

Water pollution is one major concern for streams, rivers, wetlands, and the surrounding ocean waters of Trinidad and Tobago. Various substances enter these bodies of water and affect marine life. With population growth, tourism, and business development, pollution is increasing, and in some areas, raw sewage ends up in the rivers and ocean through various sources of drainage. Industry also contributes oil pollutants, water treatment wastes, solid wastes, pesticides, and fertilizers, which alter water temperatures and in some cases are related to reef degradation. Furthermore, many pollutants cause oxygen depletion in the water, resulting in the death of certain marine organisms.

Several pollutants are known to clog fish gills, which causes significant fish deaths, as documented in the Gulf of Paria. Typical dangers to fish life include discarded plastics, oil, and other chemicals. Mangrove swamps and wetlands are also affected. They form a vital part of the marine system, providing breeding grounds for many fish and shellfish. When these areas are polluted, however, the fish and shellfish end up being unable to breed, and their population decreases.

## AIR CONTAMINATION

Trinidad and Tobago has traditionally been one of the major oil-producing countries in the world. While the oil industry has become less significant compared to the natural gas industry, it still serves a major purpose in the country today.

Several oil-producing countries, including Trinidad and Tobago, are responsible for emitting the largest amounts of carbon dioxide per person, or per capita. In 2017, Trinidad and Tobago was rated second in the world for carbon dioxide emissions per capita, averaging 33 tons (30 metric tons) per person. The only country with higher emissions was Qatar, at 54 tons (49 metric tons) per person.

Carbon dioxide is one of the primary greenhouse gases that contribute to global warming. Although Trinidad and Tobago's national output of greenhouse gases is high, the primary cause is heavy industrial processes and not the

*In May 2019, a cancer warning was reported in the* Trinidad Express *regarding seafood from the Gulf of Paria, the semi-enclosed body of water between Venezuela and the west coast of Trinidad. The area was the center of a major oil spill in 2013. The article reported that a first-time study done by the University of Trinidad and Tobago (UTT) and the University of the West Indies (UWI) claimed that seafood harvested from heavily industrialized areas along Trinidad's west coast presents "a higher cancer risk to the human population."*

Drilling sites, like this one at the Gulf of Paria, can lead to dangerous and even deadly oil spills.

*These results confirmed what local environmentalists, such as Fishermen Friends of the Sea (FFOS), had been saying for years: that there were dangerous cancer-causing substances called PAHs (polycyclic aromatic hydrocarbons) and other hazards related to the petrochemical industry present in the Gulf of Paria. The researchers found that eating seafood from the area puts about 14 percent of the Trinidad and Tobago population at risk of developing health problems each year. They also suggested remedial action to lower cancer risks or other effects to the population and marine life.*

general population. On an individual basis, residential emissions are about one-tenth of those produced by countries such as the United States and Canada; still, emissions in the region are high.

Air pollution may be a contributor to short-term health problems such as itchy eyes, nose, and throat; wheezing; coughing; shortness of breath; chest pain; headaches; nausea; and upper respiratory infections (bronchitis and pneumonia). Long-term effects include lung cancer, cardiovascular disease, chronic respiratory illnessess, and allergies. Exposure to air pollution can also be associated with heart attacks and strokes.

*Congestion on Trinidad and Tobago's roads has reached epidemic levels—as of 2019, there were over 1 million cars operating in the country. Traffic patterns and driving habits force drivers to carefully prepare if they want to reach their destination on time. Due to traffic and transportation issues, many businesses have difficulty operating properly, since employees as well as owners often arrive later than the companies' opening times. Workers typically leave their homes at least 45 minutes earlier just to get to work, and they spend an average of 45 minutes to an hour in traffic either way.*

There are many traffic jams in major cities of Trinidad and Tobago, such as Port of Spain, pictured here.

*One solution to traffic jams has been the introduction of another form of transportation, the water taxi. This kind of vehicle is able to take many commuters at one time to other areas of the country via water. Currently, water taxis operate between San Fernando and Port of Spain. Integrating such systems has helped ease congestion and encouraged more commuters to leave their cars at home.*

*Trinidad and Tobago once had a railway line, based in Trinidad, but it closed in the mid-20th century. There have been attempts, though, to resurrect a rail service in the 21st century. For instance, on April 11, 2008, the Trinitrain Consortium announced that it would plan and build a 65.2-mile (105 km), two-line Trinidad Rapid Railway. The project was scrapped in 2010 under Prime Minister Patrick Manning. In 2015, the project was reinitiated; however, in 2016, the project was once again scrapped due to falling oil prices affecting Trinidad and Tobago's economy. Perhaps a time will come when rail travel is an option for the country, but in the meantime, residents and visitors must make do with the options they have.*

# CONSERVATION EFFORTS

While Trinidad and Tobago's environment faces many challenges due to climate change and global warming, there are several conservation organizations dedicated to creating sustainability programs that work to lower carbon emissions, reverse harmful effects on the environment, and restore beauty to the islands. These organizations are also aiding in Trinidad and Tobago's commitment to various environmental protection pacts, such as the Paris Climate Agreement, which seeks to lower Earth's global temperature by 2030.

Nature Seekers is a community-based organization formed in 1990 to protect nesting leatherback turtles in Trinidad and Tobago. Its main conservation efforts are based around providing tour guide services for visitors to Matura Beach, tagging turtles for tracking, and patrolling the beach to protect the turtles and their nests, although the group's goals have also expanded to include advocating for reforestation and beach cleanup. In addition, the group has demonstrated the importance of community involvement in these efforts and has strengthened the ecotourism industry in Trinidad.

Environment TOBAGO is a nonprofit organization that focuses on awareness, advocacy, research, and conservation of local and regional ecosystems. The organization, which was established in 1996, runs programs that educate and motivate students while also contributing to the country's Sustainable Development Goals, which are part of the global effort to reduce carbon emissions and make Earth a more habitable place. The group also runs eco-focused camps over the summer and Easter holidays and trains Tobagonian schoolteachers about environmental advocacy and conservation.

# RECYCLE AND REUSE

In its 2009 budget statement, the government of Trinidad and Tobago announced that it had decided to focus on a general waste recycling system. The Trinidad and Tobago government sought the assistance of the Canadian province of Nova Scotia to draft legislation for the new system, which would create a new independent statutory waste authority under the wing of the Ministry of Local

Government, empower the waste authority to issue regulations on creating a deposit-return system for several streams of recyclables, and provide for the creation of a nationwide system of collection depots for recyclables. As of 2019, several cities had been introduced to curbside recycling systems as a further method for easy recycling. There were also plans to introduce a Beverage Container Bill, making it mandatory for all to recycle bottles and other plastic containers.

In 2015, the Environmental Management Authority (EMA), a government agency that writes and enforces laws as well as conserves the country's natural resources, began a recycling project called the Recyclable Solid Waste Collection Project. Its mission was to promote recycling of waste products throughout the country and reduce the amount of waste being sent to landfills. Initially, its main goal was to encourage the recycling of plastic bottles, though it later expanded its focus to the recycling of other materials, including e-waste, or outdated electronic products. The recycling project is meant to benefit future generations by creating a recycling culture that would make Trinidad and Tobago the Caribbean hub for recyclables.

## WATER SECURITY AND WASTE MANAGEMENT

Trinidad and Tobago is part of the United Nations (UN) Millennium Development Goals (MDG). This initiative, begun in 2002, works toward bettering the livelihood of people, animals, and plants within dedicated countries by the year 2030. Each country has its own goals. Some of Trinidad and Tobago's are ensuring environmental sustainability and providing adequate access to safe drinking water and sanitation facilities for its population. Although it comes at varying levels of service, 95 percent of the population today has access to drinking water, and about 92 percent of the population has sanitation coverage through a diverse range of waste disposal systems.

A new initiative, called Vision 2030, was put forward in 2016. This 14-year plan, inclusive of the UN MDG and Sustainable Development Goals, would see Trinidad and Tobago further improving water security and waste management across the nation.

## PLANTS AND ANIMALS

On Trinidad and Tobago's shores as well as in the waters that surround them, plants and animals abound. There are about 100 species of mammals, approximately 2,500 plant species, 70 species of freshwater fish, over 1,000 species of marine fish, 35 species of amphibians, and over 100 species of reptiles.

The Trinidad piping guan is extremely endangered. Here it is perched in a tree in one of the country's rain forests.

**TRINIDAD PIPING GUAN**   The Trinidad piping guan, also known as the pawi, is a bird species found only on Trinidad. Critically endangered and close to extinction, this large bird measures 24 inches (60 centimeters) in length and has a wingspan of 14 inches (35 cm). It has a thin neck and small head. Trinidad piping guans are forest birds. They feed on fruits and berries and build their nests in trees. The female lays three large white eggs, and she incubates them alone.

The Trinidad piping guan is mainly black with a purple gloss, or shine. Its large crest is blackish and edged with white, and it has large white wing patches. Its bare face and wattle are blue, and its legs are red. Its call is a thin piping. Its wings make a whirring sound in flight.

**WEST INDIAN MANATEE**   The West Indian manatee has adapted fully to an aquatic lifestyle, having no hind limbs with which to raise itself from the waters. The average West Indian manatee is about 8 to 13 feet (2.5 to 4 m) long and weighs between 660 and 1,100 pounds (300 and 500 kg), with females generally being larger than males. As its name implies, the West Indian manatee lives in the West Indies, or Caribbean, generally in shallow coastal areas, rivers, and estuaries. The West Indian manatee can move easily between freshwater and saltwater environments, but it prefers freshwater. It is limited to the tropics and subtropics due to an extremely low metabolic rate and lack of a thick layer of blubber—insulating body fat. West Indian manatees often are seen doing rolls, doing somersaults, and even swimming upside-down, as they are surprisingly agile in water.

Large adult manatees consume about 4 to 9 percent of their body weight each day, eating mostly sea grasses and other wet plant life. Because manatees feed on abrasive plants, their molars, or back teeth, are often worn down and are continually replaced throughout life.

The West Indian manatee has been hunted for hundreds of years for its meat and hide, or skin, and it continues to be hunted to this day. Poaching, or illegal kidnapping and killing of animals, and collisions with speeding motorboats are two of the biggest causes of manatee deaths. There is also a decline in manatee population due to the manatee's low reproductive rate.

**West Indian manatees can be found in Trinidad and Tobago and in other parts of the Caribbean.**

**LEATHERBACK SEA TURTLE**   The leatherback sea turtle is the largest of all living sea turtles and one of the largest living reptiles. Some grow to be over 7 feet (2.1 m) long and weigh more than 2,000 pounds (900 kg). It can easily be differentiated from other modern sea turtles by its lack of a hard, bony shell. Leatherback sea turtles also have long front flippers, making them powerful movers in the water.

The leatherback sea turtle's endangered status is listed as vulnerable, meaning it is at risk of becoming critically endangered and possibly extinct if its numbers continue to decline. Poachers and others who hunt the leatherback value it for its eggs, meat, and skin. People around the world still harvest sea turtle eggs. Asian exploitation of turtle nests has been cited as one of the most significant factors for the global population decline of the species. Sometimes leatherback sea turtles are also unintentionally caught in fishing nets due to commercial methods of fishing. Pollution—both chemical and physical—can also be fatal. Many turtles die from ingesting plastics that resemble their jellyfish prey. Climate change also has an adverse effect on the leatherbacks, limiting their numbers.

# NATIONAL PARKS AND PROTECTED PLACES

Trinidad and Tobago is home to many parks and reserves, or protected areas, where some of its more vulnerable animals and plants live.

A flock of great egrets flies in the Caroni Swamp Bird Sanctuary.

**ASA WRIGHT NATURE CENTER**    The Asa Wright Nature Center and Lodge, established in 1967, is a nonprofit nature resort and a scientific research station in the Arima and Aripo Valleys of the Northern Range in Trinidad. This center is one of the top bird-watching spots in the Caribbean and is also a popular destination for students studying tropical ecology. More than 160 bird species can be found at the center, including the crested oropendola, channel-billed toucan, and ornate hawk-eagle. Many butterflies, bats, and reptiles, as well as mammals like the agouti and nine-banded armadillo, can also be seen here.

**CARONI SWAMP BIRD SANCTUARY**    The Caroni Swamp is 12,000 acres (4,850 ha) and located on the west coast of Trinidad. The Caroni Swamp Bird Sanctuary is an important tourist attraction at Caroni Swamp. It provides an important habitat for the scarlet ibis, one of the national birds of Trinidad and Tobago. Other birds found here include the great egret and the flamingo.

**NARIVA SWAMP**    The Nariva Swamp is over 23 square miles (60 sq km) and is the largest mangrove freshwater wetland in Trinidad and Tobago. The swamp also is home to Bush Bush Wildlife Sanctuary, which includes over 200 species of birds and other animals. It is threatened by rice cultivation in the northwest and watermelon cultivation in the southwest. It has also been affected by deforestation.

**POINTE-À-PIERRE WILDFOWL TRUST**    Founded in 1966, the Pointe-à-Pierre Wildfowl Trust is a nonprofit nongovernment organization dedicated to environmental education and the conservation of wetlands and waterfowl.

Located in Pointe-à-Pierre, on the island of Trinidad, the trust covers about 79 acres (32 ha) and contains two lakes.

**BUCCOO REEF AND SPEYSIDE**    The Buccoo Reef, which was designated as a marine park in 1973, is the largest coral reef in Tobago. It is located near Buccoo Beach, Pigeon Point, and Store Bay. The fringing coral reefs are some of the best in the region, and because of the area's nutrient-rich coastal waters, the reefs are also home to an impressive abundance of marine life. Located close to the South American continent, Tobago is affected from the south by the Guyana Current, which carries nutrients from the Orinoco River. Plankton is produced from these nutrients, which often gives a green or brown tint to the surface waters during the rainy season (June to December). This plankton is the primary food for much of the marine life living in the coral reef. Much of it ends up as food for the massive shoals of small fry, which in turn feed large predatory fish, such as barracuda, wahoo, tarpon, and tuna. Other large animals that are frequently seen include sea turtles, reef sharks, hammerhead sharks, groupers, eagle rays, and manta rays. The rich waters are also the reason for the massive size of some of the hard corals, such as the giant brain coral off Speyside, which is over 19.7 feet (6 m) wide, and the huge barrel sponges that can be seen in the Columbus Passage south of Tobago.

**MAIN RIDGE FOREST RESERVE**    The Tobago Forest Reserve (or the Main Ridge Forest Reserve) is the oldest legally protected forest reserve in the Western Hemisphere established for a conservation purpose. It was designated as a protected British Crown reserve on April 13, 1776, following recommendations by Soame Jenyns, a member of Parliament in Great Britain who was in charge of the development of Tobago. It has remained a protected area ever since.

This forested area has great biodiversity, including 210 bird species, 16 mammal species, 24 kinds of nonpoisonous snakes, and 16 kinds of lizards. The white-tailed sabrewing hummingbird is a rare sight that flourishes in the Main Ridge Forest Reserve. It was thought to have become extinct after Hurricane Flora in 1963 but has now partially recovered its population. The

Main Ridge Forest Reserve is one of the most approachable areas of rain forest, since it is relatively small and there are certified guides who provide a diligent journey through the forest at a reasonable cost.

**LITTLE TOBAGO** Little Tobago, also known as Bird of Paradise Island, is 279 acres (113 ha) in size. The small island, located about 1.5 miles (2.4 km) off the coast of Speyside, supports some of the best dry forest remaining in the country. There are more than 50 bird species on Little Tobago and Saint Giles Island, which is the northernmost point in Trinidad and Tobago. Among them are red-billed tropicbirds, frigate birds, and Audubon's shearwaters.

Little Tobago Island, which is shown here, sits off Tobago's coast.

## INTERNET LINKS

**https://www.ema.co.tt**
This is the official Environmental Management Authority website.

**https://www.planning.gov.tt/content/land-based-pollution-drastically-affecting-tt%E2%80%99s-marine-environment**
This article touches on the pollution of coastal waters in Trinidad and Tobago, especially in the Gulf of Paria.

**https://www.planning.gov.tt/sites/default/files/NEP_Draft_1.pdf**
This is the National Environmental Policy document for the Republic of Trinidad and Tobago.

# TRINIDADIANS AND TOBAGONIANS

**There are many different people with varying ethnicities in Trinidad and Tobago.**

## 6

TRINIDAD AND TOBAGO IS HOME TO people of many different ethnicities, which makes for a country full of diversity. Everyone brings their own unique cultures to the nation, making it a place of inclusion. As of 2019, the country had over 1.3 million inhabitants. Between the two islands, Trinidad is the more populated one.

The ethnic composition of Trinidad and Tobago reflects a history of conquest and immigration. According to the last census, East Indians account for over 35 percent of the population and Africans 34 percent. People of mixed African/East Indian background make up over 7 percent of the population, while 15 percent identify as having some other mixed racial background. Other ethnicities form smaller percentages of the population.

## FIRST INHABITANTS

The tropical forest Amerindians were the first inhabitants of the islands. These indigenous, or native, groups covered a wide area of land, stretching from the upper Amazon basin in Peru to Venezuela, the Guianas, and the West Indies, and were mainly made up of the Caribs and Arawaks. Tobago was uninhabited when Christopher Columbus arrived. In the years of colonial exploitation that followed his arrival, few of Trinidad's indigenous people survived as a distinct culture, and almost all had been assimilated, or merged, into other groups by the end of the 19th century.

The Cedula of Population was a 1783 decree of the Spanish royal government related to Trinidad and Tobago. It invited anyone of the Roman Catholic faith who would swear loyalty to the Spanish Crown to take ownership of a certain amount of land free of charge, depending on their race and heritage. The decree drew many French settlers to Trinidad.

## EUROPEAN POPULATION

The Europeans were the next group of people to come to the islands—first the Spanish, then the French, and later the English, as well as small numbers of Italians and Portuguese. In the 18th and 19th centuries, these people formed the wealthy, ruling, aristocratic classes of Trinidad. The French arrived mainly during the Spanish colonization period to take advantage of free agricultural lands. The Portuguese were brought to replace freed African slaves when they refused to accept low wages.

Europeans now only make up 0.6 percent of the country's population. Many people of European descent live in areas in and around Port of Spain in Trinidad. They include people of British, French, Italian, Spanish, Portuguese, and German heritage.

## AFRICAN POPULATION

Afro-Trinidadians and Tobagonians make up the country's second-largest ethnic group—about 34 percent of its overall population. The majority of Afro-Trinidadians and Tobagonians are descendants of the former slaves who were brought to the islands in the last few years of the Spanish colonial era and the beginning of the English colonial period. They have a strong sense of cultural identity that has strongly influenced the islands.

## OTHER POPULATIONS

The largest ethnic group in the country is East Indian. They make up over 35 percent of the population. They are primarily descendants of indentured workers from India, who were brought to to replace freed African slaves who refused to continue working on the sugar plantations. Most of them are farmers who live in the rural areas; however, today many Indians also hold positions in business and politics. Many people of Indian descent have retained their religion and culture, although it has been altered by European and African influences. They are Hindu, Muslim, and Christian by religion. Indian people

## SANTA ROSA CARIB COMMUNITY

*The Santa Rosa Carib Community of Arima in Trinidad is made up of partial descendants of the original Carib-speaking inhabitants of Trinidad and Tobago. They were given official recognition as an indigenous community by the state in May 1990. Their main goal in forming this group was to keep the spirit of the indigenous peoples alive. Some of the cultural traditions this group maintains are in horticulture, cassava processing, hunting practices, house building, and weaving. The community also organizes the Santa Rosa Festival on August 23 each year. This event honors the community's patron saint, Saint Rose of Lima.*

The Santa Rosa Carib Community takes part in the First Peoples' Ceremonial Walk on the streets of Port of Spain.

tend to live as extended families, with several generations of one family living together.

The Chinese, Lebanese, and various other ethnicities make up about 1 percent of the population. In particular, the Chinese and Lebanese have been known throughout the world as traders. They have a strong presence in the chief towns of Trinidad and Tobago, and the Chinese often run the small shops in the villages. There are many people living in Trinidad and Tobago who have Chinese, African, and Indian heritages.

Given the diversity of groups that have come to Trinidad and Tobago, it is no surprise that many of the nation's residents identify as being of mixed race. The country's last census divided this share of the population into two groups: people of mixed East Indian and African ancestry, and people with other mixed backgrounds. In total, people of mixed backgrounds make up about 23 percent of the country's population. Of these, about one-third identify as African/East Indian.

## REFUGEES

*More than 4 million citizens of Venezuela, which amounts to over 10 percent of the country's population, have emigrated to other countries. Most have left since 2015 to escape an economic and political crisis threatening the country. Some have settled in the Caribbean, in places such as Aruba, Curaçao, and Trinidad. According to Trinidadian officials, roughly 60,000 Venezuelans had settled in Trinidad by late 2018. Some of them came to the country legally as tourists and overstayed their visas. Those without passports may have paid a boat captain to transport them to the country at night.*

**Many Venezuelans have fled their country to seek refuge in Trinidad and Tobago. Here, Venezuelans wait outside an office in Port of Spain to discuss asylum.**

*In 1951, Trinidad signed the Convention Relating to the Status of Refugees, which determines international refugee law within the country. The convention is specific to asylum-seeking refugees and countries agreeing to take in asylum seekers. It lays out the rights of asylum seekers and responsibilities of those granting asylum. However, this policy is not always followed in the 21st century.*

*In April 2018, Trinidad deported a number of Venezuelan refugees, claiming there was not enough space on the island for them. In a news conference that same month, Prime Minister Keith Rowley defended the country's policy of not allowing every refugee in who seeks asylum. The United Nations Refugee Agency and other human rights groups said this was a breach of conduct. Trinidad "must respect the fundamental human right to seek asylum and never return people to countries where their lives or freedom are at risk," said Erika Guevara-Rosas, director for the Americas at Amnesty International. Trinidad has been criticized for its lack of action in helping Venezuelan migrants and has yet to institute an official asylum policy.*

## HOSPITALITY

While Trinidadians and Tobagonians tend to live in well-defined ethnic groups, they also share a distinct national character. They are known for offering their generous hospitality to visitors from other countries, especially during specific celebrations and festivals, such as Diwali (the Hindu Festival of Lights), Christmas, Carnival, and the Tobago Heritage Festival.

The celebration of Carnival originated in the late 18th century in Trinidad, when French settlers brought the Fat Tuesday masquerade party tradition to the island, and the celebration spread from there to the rest of the Caribbean. Fat Tuesday is the day before the start of Lent—a Roman Catholic time of reflection and sacrifice. Lent ends with Easter.

On national festival days, everyone celebrates, regardless of the ethnic origin of the festival. All the people of the islands share various cuisines and enjoy the national music of calypso. This music also reflects the national character in its refusal to be impressed with anyone or take anything too seriously. During tough times, the islanders have responded by throwing parties called fetes. Many fetes have been thrown during difficult economic periods to lift people's spirits and show them, despite the country's troubles, that the people of Trinidad and Tobago still know how to enjoy themselves.

In the 1970s, authorities imposed a dusk-to-dawn curfew in Trinidad due to violence in the country. To combat these curfews, Trinidadians hosted indoor curfew fetes, which started before the curfew would start and ended the next morning when the curfew ended.

## INTERNET LINKS

**http://www.caribbean-atlas.com/en/themes/waves-of-colonization-and-control-in-the-caribbean/waves-of-colonization/trinidad-1498-1962.html**
This website provides information on the history of the different types of people who settled on the islands.

**https://www.gotrinidadandtobago.com/trinidad-and-tobago/culture-in-trinidad-and-tobago.html**
This website provides information on some of the different cultural groups that exist in Trinidad and Tobago and the holidays they celebrate.

**https://www.nationsencyclopedia.com/Americas/Trinidad-and-Tobago-ETHNIC-GROUPS.html**
This website gives a brief overview of the different ethnic groups present on Trinidad and Tobago.

# LIFESTYLE

Shown here is a man wearing a Rastafarian-style hat on the streets of Scarborough, Tobago.

## 7

THERE ARE VARIOUS CULTURES comprising the people of Trinidad and Tobago, but they all face many of the same challenges despite their different lifestyles. Citizens today face issues such as those relating to the climate, economic conditions, life expectancy, education, and health care. These issues challenge them to think of new ways of advancing in the 21st century.

## BLACK CULTURE

Afro-Trinidadians are united by their ethnicity and common heritage. Their ancestors arrived on the islands as slaves, either directly in slave ships that brought them from the west coast of Africa, often Ghana, or as slaves of settlers from other Caribbean islands.

Many aspects of African life have remained within the overall cultural makeup of Trinidad and Tobago's residents. African religions have influenced Trinidad's religions, and the rhythms of African music can be heard in the sounds of Carnival. Afro-Trinidadians left the countryside after emancipation. This group is mostly urban and has received a good education. Their religions are often new forms of Christianity, and there are large numbers of believers in Rastafarianism, a religion developed in Jamaica in the 1930s.

In Trinidad and Tobago, there continue to be aspects of racism. However, what Westerners would call racist, many Trinidadians think of as normal and accepted behavior. Trinidadians discuss skin tone and racial characteristics in a way that people from many other societies do not.

In the 1970s, a particular style of dressing emerged associated with the black power movement in the United States, which some Trinidadians and Tobagonians adopted. It featured Afro hairstyles and loose, brightly patterned African shirts. Today, however, men wear casual T-shirts and pants in their leisure time. For the office, a tie and short-sleeved shirt are more common.

## INDIAN CULTURE

For a hundred years or more, the Indian population of Trinidad and Tobago consisted of poorly educated field workers, but as education has improved over the decades, a demographic change has been taking place, with Indians moving into middle-class, white-collar jobs and into the cities to work.

Many Indian businessmen still have ties with their families in India. They also strongly maintain their ties to their heritage and have kept many traditions and ways of life from India. Indian celebrations, foods, and religions have become an important part of the Trinidadian and Tobagonian cultural landscape.

This woman is looking at some of the Indian street food offered in Trinidad and Tobago.

## WHITE CULTURE

Some privileged white citizens of Trinidad and Tobago have lives that are very different from those of other people living in this country. Their children attend private schools run by religious orders, and they live in large private estates in the countryside. Their leisure activities separate them from ordinary Trinidadians and Tobagonians, as do their jobs, which are typically in higher management.

## CITY LIVING

Trinidad and Tobago only has two main cities—Port of Spain and San Fernando in Trinidad. Business hours in these two cities are typically from 8:00 a.m. to 4:00 p.m.; however, some stores stay open late in the evening and on the weekend. Port of Spain is the administrative center of the islands, and many civil service workers live there. Besides being a center for administration and banking, Port of Spain is an industrial base, with many of its citizens working in sawmills, textile mills, citrus canneries, and the Angostura bitters factory. The city has a major port, which makes it a center for trade within the West Indies. San Fernando, located in the oil fields and south of Port of Spain, is an administrative and trading center for the southern part of Trinidad. Many people living in San Fernando work in the oil industry.

## CITY HOUSING

Just over 53 percent of the population in Trinidad and Tobago live in urban areas. Most of the housing in Trinidadian cities is made of wood. Houses in the suburbs of Port of Spain are located in the hills behind the city, with steeply sloping yards. Houses are small, often one-story buildings with corrugated iron roofs, but they are in shady areas lined with fruit trees and have a sufficient supply of clean water and electricity. As people have grown wealthier, they have added on more stories to their houses, which take on a strange, impromptu form as they expand upward. Individual suburbs were developed for the various ethnic

**Farmers sell their goods at a marketplace in Scarborough.**

groups and are still largely racially divided. Among the simpler constructed buildings, huge brick houses, built in many different styles, stand out. Most of them are in the center of cities like Port of Spain and are still privately owned or have become government offices.

## SHOPPING

Although Trinidad and Tobago has a fair share of supermarkets where people go to buy expensive imports from the United States, it also has flourishing street markets, such as the Arima Market, Santa Cruz Green Market, San Fernando Market, and Tunapuna Market, where people can buy fresh local produce.

Fruit, vegetable, and fish stalls line the streets and harbors of the cities. While some of the street markets are highly regulated covered markets, others are little shantytowns where the vendors have built rickety buildings along the street or inside unused building sites. Many of the stallholders actually live on the premises, and small villages have sprung up within the cities, populated by the stallholders. Craft markets also spring up in tourist areas. Cooked food stalls line the streets as well, selling ready-made Chinese, Indian, and Trinidadian meals to office workers.

Trinidad also has some of the largest shopping malls in the Caribbean, such as The Falls at Westmall, Long Circular Mall, and Trincity Mall. These shopping centers attract visitors from other islands and surrounding regions too. Many stores import products from Venezuela, China, Brazil, and the United States.

## COUNTRY LIVING

Nearly 47 percent of the population of Trinidad and Tobago lives in rural areas, the majority of which are located in the south of Trinidad or in the west of the island around Arouca. Some live in Tobago, which has virtually no big industries. The rural people in Tobago either farm or work in the tourism industry or in the local government.

Life on the big estates is hard, and most estate workers are poor. Most people live in small, single-story wooden huts with tin roofs and often a large overhanging veranda to shield them from the harsh sun. They supplement their income with their own fruit and vegetable gardens.

## LIVING IN TOBAGO

Life in Tobago is slow and easygoing, with tiny villages spread out around the countryside, compared to Trinidad, which is busy, noisy, polluted in places, and full of congested roads. The majority of people in Tobago work on their own small farms or in tourism. Buildings include the expensive country homes of wealthy Trinidadians and the more modest homes of the local people. Roads are narrow and largely unpaved, and some disappear during a bad rainy season.

Though Tobago has a more rural feel, it does not lack the dynamic energy of Trinidad. Indeed, Tobago has its own Carnival, which focuses on the theatrical and folk elements of this special occasion. The island has many other rural festivals as well. Most of these are Christian in origin. The only town of any size

In 2015, Prime Minister Keith Rowley greeted students from Bishop's High School at his swearing-in ceremony at Queen's Hall in Port of Spain.

on Tobago is Scarborough, and it resembles a small country town in Europe rather than a typical thriving capital city.

## SCHOOLING AND HEALTH CARE

In Trinidad and Tobago, about 99 percent of the population is literate. Education is free and mandatory between the ages of 5 and 16. The government provides students with free transport, books, and meals. Trinidad and Tobago is one of the most educated countries in the Caribbean and the world.

There are about 500 primary schools on the islands and 200 secondary schools. Secondary education is based on the old British system, where an examination taken at the age of 12 draws out the top students to grammar schools, while those who do not pass the test attend a secondary school where the emphasis is on technical subjects.

There are three universities in Trinidad and Tobago: the University of Trinidad and Tobago, the University of the Southern Caribbean, and the University of the West Indies. The universities all offer degree courses in engineering, law, medicine, education, agriculture, liberal arts, natural sciences, and social sciences. In addition, there are a number of other technical colleges, teacher training colleges, and educational institutes. Wealthier students who can afford the fees tend to go to college in the United States. Some private schools are run by Christian groups.

Children generally start preschool between three and five years old. Although it is not mandatory for children to start school at the age of three, most Trinidadians and Tobagonians start their children's education at this stage because children are expected to have basic reading and writing skills when they begin primary school.

*Acquired immunodeficiency syndrome (AIDS) is a sexually transmitted disease caused by the human immunodeficiency virus (HIV) that has affected millions of people around the world. In the 1980s and 1990s, it killed many people. In the 21st century, it still exists. The HIV/AIDS epidemic that has plagued the world for decades continues to be a problem throughout Trinidad and Tobago. At the end of 2015, there were between 10,000 and 11,000 people living with HIV in the country. Since the start of the epidemic in 1983, the general public has not been provided with adequate education, resources, and support to fight the disease. There are also deterrents many Trinidadians and Tobagonians face when going to get tested for the disease, such as dealing with staff who are not properly trained to handle sensitive issues, space constraints where patients' privacy is revealed to others due to thin-walled rooms, and delays in receiving laboratory tests for HIV/AIDS. Several organizations, such as UNAIDS, are working to end AIDS as a public health threat by 2030.*

In 2018, the infant mortality rate in Trinidad and Tobago was 16 deaths per 1,000 live births, a better average than most Caribbean countries. There are about 3 doctors for every 1,000 people. Life expectancy is around 73 years. The leading cause of death is heart disease, while this along with various cancers, diabetes, and stroke account for 60 percent of all deaths in the country. The government runs a free public health-care program as well as a compulsory retirement pension plan, and there are benefits for maternity leave, sickness, and industrial injury. About 26 percent of the population lives below the poverty line.

## GETTING AROUND

There are several forms of transportation citizens, residents, and visitors can use to get around. The most popular public options are the government-run bus service (known as the Public Transport Service Corporation, or PTSC) and privately owned minibuses (locally known as maxi-taxis); however, privately

The ticket for the 25-minute flight between Port of Spain and Tobago costs $25 (in US dollars) for one way or $50 for a round trip.

There are ferries, such as this one, that transport passengers between Port of Spain and Scarborough.

owned cars are also common. Maxi-taxis and some cars carry passengers along fixed routes for a fare. There are also ferries that operate between Port of Spain and Scarborough. Cars can be brought onto the ferries and kept in the cargo areas. Domestic flights between Port of Spain's Piarco International Airport and Tobago's A. N. R. Robinson International Airport have been operated by Caribbean Airlines since October 2007.

## GETTING MARRIED

Most Afro-Trinidadians in Trinidad and Tobago enter a committed relationship before deciding to get married. They may live together or may not. Some enter a common-law marriage, or a marriage without an official ceremony and based on the number of years people have been living together. Others eventually have a formal marriage ceremony. The most popular form of this kind of ceremony is a civil marriage performed by a licensed individual. Most couples prefer a traditional-style wedding, with the bride in a white dress and the groom in a black suit.

Hindu weddings within the Indian community are traditional. In the past, marriages were arranged between families, typically with someone of the same caste, or social class. Today, more people are choosing who they want to marry.

Here are a bride and groom dressed in traditional wedding attire during a Hindu wedding ceremony in Trinidad and Tobago.

## INTERNET LINKS

**https://borgenproject.org/top-10-facts-about-living-conditions-in -trinidad-and-tobago**
This blog offers up interesting facts about lifestyle and culture in Trinidad and Tobago.

**https://www.everyculture.com/To-Z/Trinidad-and-Tobago.html**
This website discusses the lifestyle, history, geography, and other aspects of Trinidad and Tobago.

RELIGION

Shown here is a Catholic church in Port
of Spain, Trinidad, around 1895.

## 8

T HERE ARE SEVERAL DIFFERENT religions throughout Trinidad and Tobago, and many ethnic groups practice their own religion. However, out of all the religions in the nation, Christianity is the most widely practiced. Most Trinidadians and Tobagonians are accepting of those who think differently than them, and everyone is welcome to take part in all religious festivals and celebrations.

## RELIGIOUS NUMBERS

Among Trinidadians and Tobagonians, over 32 percent of the total population are of the Protestant faith. However, they are split into several different denominations, or types, including Pentecostal or evangelical Christian (12 percent of the population), Baptist or Spiritual/Shouter Baptist (6.9 percent), Anglican (5.7 percent), Seventh-Day Adventist (4.1 percent), Presbyterian or Congregational (2.5 percent), Methodist (0.7 percent), and Moravian (0.3 percent), according to the last census. Meanwhile, Roman Catholic Christians make up 21.6 percent of the population, while Jehovah's Witnesses account for 1.5 percent.

Among the Indian population are Hindus, making up 18.2 percent of the total population. In addition, Muslims make up 5 percent. There are

also traditional Caribbean religious groups with African roots, such as the followers of Orisha (0.9 percent), who mix West African spiritualism and Christianity. The Shouter Baptist branch of Protestant Christianity also incorporates African influences.

Religious groups such as Baha'is, Rastafarians, Buddhists, Jews, and small Christian groups, including the Church of Jesus Christ of Latter-Day Saints, fall under the "other" category and make up 7.5 percent of the total population. Those who have no religious affiliation make up 2.2 percent, while 11.1 percent did not report a religious affiliation to the census.

## CHRISTIANITY

There are many forms of Christianity in Trinidad and Tobago. Although there are more Protestants than Catholics in the nation, Catholics make up the largest single Christian group. The tenets, or main points, of Roman Catholicism are the belief in the Holy Trinity (that God is made up of Father, Son, and Holy Spirit); the veneration of, or respect for, Mary, the mother of Jesus; and the belief in transubstantiation, or the blessing of the bread and wine that Catholics believe become the real body and blood of Jesus during the service, called the Mass.

Hinduism is one of the top religions practiced in Trinidad and Tobago. Here, a Hindu woman is praying at a Hindu temple in Port of Spain.

The Anglican Church is very close in ideology and ritual to Roman Catholicism. Both have ornately decorated churches, and in both the priesthood determines church policy, although Anglicans do not recognize the pope, who leads the Roman Catholic Church. Instead, the leader of the Anglican church is the British monarch (king or queen). In addition, Holy Communion is treated as simply a symbol of the body and blood of Christ in the Anglican Church. In both churches, worship takes place on Sundays.

Another Christian denomination, the Presbyterian Church, originated in Scotland and is governed by a body of laymen, or people who are not professional priests.

## ORISHA WORSHIP

The slaves who came to Trinidad and Tobago brought with them elements of their original African religious beliefs. On the islands, these beliefs mixed with Christianity. Many people of African descent on the islands practice Orisha, a religion largely found in Tobago. In this form of worship, participants believe that besides an all-powerful God, there are spirits that exist in everything around them. This is also known as animism. In order to pacify, or please, and even to get help from these spirits, one must worship them through ritual dances, offerings, drumbeats, chanting, singing, and prayer.

Orisha originated among the Yoruba—African people who once inhabited an area from Benin to the Niger River but who now live largely in Nigeria. During British rule in Trinidad and Tobago, the religion was suppressed, and thus its practice became secretive. It remains so today. The most notable animist god is Shango, the god of fire, thunder, and lightning, who is depicted carrying an *oshe*, a double-headed battle-ax. Shango is also recognized in parts of Cuba and Haiti, and some traditions merge Shango's story with that of Christianity's Saint Barbara.

Other deities of the Orisha religion include Ogun, the warrior god of iron and steel; Oshun, goddess of water and beauty; and Osain, Yoruba god of herbal medicine, healing, and prophecy.

Orisha worship takes place in a palais, which is often a sheltered courtyard partly covered by a galvanized roof and decorated with the symbols of individual spirits—weapons, jugs of water, and the materials used during worship, such as foods, olive oil, and flowers.

This is a ceramic ritual pot for the goddess Oshun, who is worshipped in the Orisha religion.

## SHOUTER BAPTISTS

Spiritual Baptism, a form of Christianity that came to the islands through former American slaves in the 19th century, is another form of worship. It encompasses many outward signs of expression, such as shouting. Thus, worshippers were sometimes called "shouters." Because of this, the religion was banned in Trinidad and Tobago between 1917 and 1951. The ban was lifted on March 30, 1951, which the Spiritual Baptists celebrate as Shouter Baptist Liberation Day.

The basis of the faith is the worship of the Holy Trinity—Father, Son, and Holy Spirit—but like Orisha, this faith recognizes animist spirits that must be pacified. Outwardly, a Shouter Baptist church looks like any other Christian church, with an altar and rows of benches called pews. However, these churches include a center pole from which symbolic objects, such as flowers, jugs of water, and candles, are hung to attract the animist spirits. Members of the church dress up on Sundays in long white robes and colorful head wraps to attend services that can last up to six hours. The service begins with purification rituals to cast out any unpleasant spirits known as jumbies that might be in the church. Lighted candles are placed in front of doors and windows, incense is burned, and brass bells are rung. The service proceeds with readings from the Bible to the rhythmic clapping of hands. Similar to followers of Orisha, members of the congregation believe they become possessed by spirits and shout out loud, often speaking in tongues, an uttering of incomprehensible sounds that the speaker believes is a deity speaking through him or her.

**A worshipper dances during a celebration of Shouter Baptist Liberation Day in 2011.**

## RASTAFARI

Rastafari, also known as Rastafarianism, originated in Jamaica in the 1930s out of Ethiopianism and Pan-Africanism, which was advocated by political figure Marcus Garvey. This form of worship has become popular in Trinidad in recent years. It is an Abrahamic religion (based on the teachings of Abraham, a biblical figure) with influences from Judaism, Christianity, and Islam. Rastafarians have their own version of the Bible called the Holy Piby, or the Black Man's Bible. Rastafarians believe that the late emperor of Ethiopia, Haile Selassie I, was a descendant of the biblical King Solomon and view him as a modern messiah. The religion takes its name from Selassie's original name, Ras (Prince) Tafari. Their name for God is "Jah."

Rastafarians believe Haile Selassie I, who ruled Ethiopia from 1930 to 1974, is the black messiah and related to King Solomon.

Rastafarians do not eat processed food, salt, meat, or dairy products, and they do not use any stimulants, or substances that keep a person awake, although marijuana is used during prayer meetings or meditation. Some of those who practice the religion believe that all black people should return to Ethiopia. Rastafarians typically wear long dreadlocks, in keeping with the Bible's exhortation, "They shall not make baldness upon their head, neither shall they shave off the corner of their beard."

## HINDU WORSHIP

Hinduism was introduced in Trinidad and Tobago by Indian indentured workers, but after 170 years, it has changed quite a lot from the religion that is practiced in India.

Hinduism is a major world religion comprised of multiple systems of philosophy, belief, and ritual. Hindus worship a number of gods, including Shiva, the god of destruction who is one of the religion's most important gods. Brahma is the god of creation—another very important Hindu god. Next in importance is Vishnu, who has four arms and is said to be the preserver of life. Vishnu takes on new forms, known as avatars, in order to save Earth from various damages. The elephant-headed god, Ganesha, is the god of beginnings and is worshipped at the start of rites and ceremonies. Lakshmi, the goddess of wealth and good fortune, is worshipped at the Diwali festival. Other gods are Durga, a goddess of war, and Sarasvati, the goddess of learning and the arts.

Unlike Hinduism in India, the version in Trinidad and Tobago has almost no vestige of the caste system, a traditional system based on a person's social status used in India. In India, people marry and accept employment within their caste, but on the islands, the caste system is of less importance.

A Hindu religious service on the islands is also different from services in India. The service takes place in the temple as it would in India, but the service, called a *puja* (PU-ja), combines the worship of several deities at once; in India, the puja is dedicated to only one deity. During the service, the priest arranges offerings such as flowers, oil, herbs, and pictures of the deities. Then, the pandit, a teacher skilled in Hinduism, blesses the arrangements and anoints

A young girl lights candles called *deyas* as part of celebrating Diwali.

a flagpole. The deities' flags are raised, symbolizing the blessing of the building and the participants. Hindus in Trinidad and Tobago celebrate Diwali, the Festival of Lights, and Phagwa, or Holi as it's also called, the spring festival.

## THE ISLAMIC RELIGION

Islam originated in seventh-century Arabia through the Prophet Muhammad. Its followers are known as Muslims, and the religion affects almost every aspect of their lives. It is based on five pillars: profession of faith, performance of prayer, giving of alms, observance of fasting, and a pilgrimage to Mecca, a sacred city in Saudi Arabia.

The profession of faith can be summed up by these words: "There is no deity but God, and Muhammad is the messenger of God." In Islam, the name for God is "Allah." The sacred scripture of Islam, which discusses the will of Allah, is called the Quran. According to Muslims, there are many other prophets, including Jesus Christ, but Muhammad is the most important.

Muslims must pray at least five times a day: at dawn, before sunrise; at midday, after the sun passes its highest point; in the late part of the afternoon; directly after sunset; and before bed, between sunset and midnight. Prayers can be done outside, inside, or at specific worship houses called mosques. A distinctive architectural feature of mosques all over the world as well as in Trinidad and Tobago is the minaret. From this tower-like structure, a person called the muezzin calls the worshippers to prayer. All worshippers face the holy city of Mecca.

Muslims are expected to give a portion of their annual salary, known as zakat, to the poor. During the holy month of Ramadan, when practicing Muslims fast, no food, drink, or tobacco may be consumed between sunrise and sunset. Children begin to take part in the annual fast at about the age when they reach puberty. The fifth pillar of the faith is the pilgrimage, or hajj, to Mecca. All Muslims are expected to complete it at least once in their life.

The two branches of Islam, Shia and Sunni, are split due to a disagreement over the succession of Muhammad after his death in 632. One group believed only descendants of Muhammad should be able to take over leading the Muslim community. They supported Ali, the cousin and son-in-law of Muhammad, and became known as the Shia sect. Another group wanted more freedom to choose a new leader. They supported one of Muhammad's closest friends, Abu Bakr, and became known as the Sunni sect.

Muslims in Trinidad and Tobago celebrate the annual Eid al-Fitr festival, which marks the end of Ramadan, along with several other Muslim holidays.

Followers of Islam can worship at this mosque in Port of Spain.

## SUPERSTITIONS

Many people in Trinidad and Tobago believe in superstitions. Jumbies, or *dih* (DEE) to the Indians, come in many forms.

*Douens* (DOO-ens) are the malevolent spirits of unbaptized children. Their faces with no features are hidden under straw hats, and their feet point backward. They supposedly lurk where living children play. Parents who believe in these spirits seldom speak their children's names aloud for fear that the douens might learn them and harm the children.

The *lugarhoo* (LOO-gar-who) is a mythical shape-shifting monster that feeds on fresh blood. The sound of rattling chains signals its arrival, as the creature is said to drag them behind it. Superstitious people often hang a pair

*There are various legends that are part of Trinidadian and Tobagonian folklore, such as the stories of the origin of Pitch Lake. One story involves Callifaria, the daughter of Callisuna, the chief of the La Brea tribe. She flees from her village to find her lover, Kasaka, who is prince of the rival Cumana tribe. Her upset father attacks the Cumana tribe and captures and ties his daughter to a horse, forcing her to return home. Pimlontas, a winged god, becomes angry at Callisuna and causes the La Brea village to sink into the ground, covering it with a thick black substance called piche, creating Pitch Lake.*

*Another story of the creation of Pitch Lake involves the Chiman tribe that lived on the site of the lake. In the story, the Chiman win a battle and celebrate with a feast of hummingbirds, which are protected by the gods. In retribution, the winged god opens up the earth, creating Pitch Lake. The Chiman tribe are swallowed up by the earth in the process.*

of open scissors in the shape of the crucifix over the bed, as well as a Bible at the head of the bed, to ward off the lugarhoo. These symbols of Christianity are thought to protect the people living in a household haunted by the lugarhoo.

A *soucouyant* (SUE-koo-ant) is a female vampire that takes the form of a reclusive old woman and lives in villages among the people. At night, she travels around as a ball of fire searching for victims, keeping her skin in a mortar bowl while she flies until daybreak. If the skin is found, covering it with salt is supposed to prevent her from getting back into it.

## OBEAH

Obeah is a form of sorcery or witchcraft practiced in certain cultures in the Caribbean. This spiritual and healing practice developed among enslaved West Africans in the West Indies. Practitioners of obeah use healing techniques and rituals, as well as incantations, talismans, spells, and herbal remedies, to help those in need of curing.

Two common ways to dispense herbal remedies are through bush-baths and bush teas. In making a bush tea, the obeah selects particular herbs and other materials and boils them. The infusion is drunk. The herbs must be collected at a certain time, depending on the ailment. The cures can be for physical or mental illnesses. Some herbs are cooling, while others are purging. Purging herbs are senna, pawpaw bark, or castor oil. The use of lemongrass, black sage, and Christmas bush is the remedy for cold. Fevers are treated with lime and Saint-John's-wort.

Some practitioners are known for their ability to extract objects from their patients' bodies. Some of the supposed objects extracted include pins, money, pencils, nails, and roaches, or various kinds of animals, such as rats, snakes, frogs, and lizards.

In many Caribbean countries, obeah has developed a stigma, or negative reputation, similar to voodoo, a religion practiced in Haiti. Obeah was first made illegal, as part of the slave codes, during the time of slavery in Trinidad, though this ban expired when slavery ended. However, Trinidad's Summary Convictions Ordinance of 1868 made obeah punishable by whipping and imprisonment for men, and whipping for women. In 2000, the term "obeah" was removed from all laws, decriminalizing the practice.

In West African folklore, obeah is also the name for a giant animal that enters villages and kidnaps girls on behalf of witches.

## INTERNET LINKS

**https://www.bbc.co.uk/religion/religions/rastafari/history/history.shtml**
This website provides information on the history of Rastafarianism.

**https://www.britannica.com/place/Trinidad-and-Tobago/People#ref275757**
Information about the various religions of Trinidad and Tobago is provided on this section from the *Encyclopedia Britannica*.

**https://classroom.synonym.com/what-do-the-spiritual-baptists-believe-12087903.html**
This article provides information on Spiritual Baptists.

**https://warwick.ac.uk/fac/arts/english/events/warvan-copy/prog/paton_trevor.pdf**
This document offers insight into the practices of obeah.

# LANGUAGE

WELCOME TO **TRINIDAD & TOBAGO**

BIENVENIDO A **TRINIDAD & TOBAGO**

Trinidad and Tobago's residents speak
many different languages.

## 9

WHEN WALKING ON THE STREETS of Trinidad and Tobago, several different variations of languages can be heard. The country's official language is English; however, many tourists might have trouble recognizing the language spoken due to its multiple dialects. In official circles, Standard English is the norm. This is a formal type of English that uses no slang. However, in casual conversation and in most informal situations, people use Trini. This is a form of English that is also based on many other languages that have seeped into the culture.

The languages spoken on both Trinidad and Tobago are derived from the combined historical influences of various indigenous cultures and settlers over the centuries.

## CREOLE LANGUAGES

When African slaves were first brought to Trinidad and Tobago, they spoke a multitude of African languages, depending on their place of origin in Africa. In order to communicate with one another and to take orders from their masters, they had to find a lingua franca, a common language that they could all understand. The slaves developed the use of pidgin, a common improvised second language, which allowed them to speak to their masters and be understood by them.

From this need emerged a creole, or mixed, language, based loosely on English but incorporating many African words and expressions. The grammar at first was probably African, with English nouns added as a common core of understanding. Each African spoke his or her own language fluently and perhaps a little bit of the other slaves' languages as well, but all their orders came in French, Spanish, or English. Therefore, over generations, the African languages slowly transformed, and the mother tongue of the slaves became a hybridized form of speech.

For about 100 years, the language spoken in Trinidad and Tobago was a creole form of French, which was basically French with words from African languages, such as Twi or Yoruba, included. Even today, there is a strong element of French in Trini, and in some rural areas people still speak a language that is closer to French than to English.

## TRINIDADIAN AND TOBAGONIAN CREOLE

Today, there are two main types of English spoken on the islands: Trinidadian Creole, also known as Trini, and Tobagonian Creole. Which one someone uses depends on whether the person is from, or resides in, Trinidad or Tobago. These forms of English have their own authentic grammar and articulation. Several of the words used in these two dialects are Standard English words that have taken on different meanings.

These languages spoken in Trinidad or Tobago, mainly derived from English, are a mixture of influences from other languages. Trini, which is most popular in Trinidad, incorporates English with African languages, French, French Creole (otherwise known as Patois), Chinese, and Trinidadian Hindustani. It is not just a collection of borrowed nouns and a few odd phrases. It has a special quality of its own that reflects the national character. For example, Trini uses many more double entendres than British or American English. One explanation for this manner of saying one thing but meaning another is that during slavery, the slaves had to be careful of what they said in front of their masters, so they developed this way of speaking.

*Many Trinbagonians, people from either Trinidad or Tobago, use expressions connected with having fun, relaxing, enjoying the festive time of Carnival, and other aspects of social life. In businesses and schools, Standard English is used, so it is only on the streets that colorful sayings, such as the following, can be heard:*

| | |
|---|---|
| *bashment* | *a big party or a festival that went really well* |
| *big up* | *bragging and praising someone else at the same time* |
| *boldfaced* | *being pushy, promoting yourself* |
| *break a lime* | *leave a party when it is at its height* |
| *catchin yuh tail.* | *down on your luck, without money* |
| *darkers* | *sunglasses* |
| *dou dou* | *sweetheart* |
| *fedupsy* | *bored* |
| *fete* | *party* |
| *hol' strain.* | *wait a moment* |
| *ignorant.* | *quick to take offense* |
| *jammin* | *working hard* |
| *liming.* | *having a good time with your friends* |
| *make style* | *to show off* |
| *ramcram* | *packed to capacity* |
| *sweetman.* | *a man who is supported by his girlfriend* |
| *Tobago love.* | *not showing your real feelings* |
| *yuh business fix* | *you're all organized now* |

Tobagonian Creole has fewer influences. It has fewer Hindi additions and is closer to a mix of African and English languages. This is the language primarily spoken in Tobago.

## FRENCH INFLUENCE

There are many French expressions and words in Trini. Most of the words that describe the jumbies of superstition are of French derivation. If someone spreads spiteful gossip about a neighbor, it is called *mauvais langue*, which translates to "bad language." The French influence is even more noticeable in Trini syntax. In French, describing the weather involves the verb *faire*, "to do" or "to make," so that a French person would say *Il fait chaud*—literally "It makes hot"—to say that the weather is hot. In Trini, French words are directly translated into English, but the structure remains French. Thus, instead of "It is hot," a Trinidadian might say "It making hot."

## HINDI INFLUENCE

The Indian workers who came to Trinidad and Tobago were different from the African slaves, as they came with a common culture and language and maintained their own language as indentured workers. Hindi, the language that most of them spoke and the fourth most spoken language in the world today, is still used in the Indian community. However, the language is rarely spoken in the workplace or at mixed social events, as younger people are more apt to speak Trini or Standard English.

East Indian workers and their families have influenced the language landscape of Trinidad and Tobago.

In 1990, Trinidad and Tobago's Parliament formed the language organization Hindi Nidhi, which seeks to promote the Hindi language in schools to establish a wider understanding and appreciation for the language among the various communities on the islands. It still exists today, establishing and overseeing many Hindi classes for students and community members alike. The organization also hosts conferences and other events.

Most of the indentured workers lived in specific rural areas of Trinidad, and their descendants still make up a large portion of the community in the south and east of the island. It is possible to see the continuing development of Trini as a language in the way that Hindi has influenced the language that is being spoken in Trinidad. Indians are still largely associated with small holdings as vegetable growers, so many of the words for vegetables have two options—one is the older English, French, or Spanish word, and the other is a newer Hindi one. In Trinidad and Tobago, the bulbous, purple vegetable that Americans call an eggplant has been known as *melongene*, from an early French word.

Now, it is also called *baingan*, from Hindi. English speakers call it "aubergine," as it is called in Britain.

## SPANISH INFLUENCE

Spanish was the original language of the first European settlers in Trinidad. A Spanish-based creole, known as Coco Payol, was once widely used on the islands. Remnants of Coco Payol are still found in everyday speech, though Spanish has left fewer marks on Trini English than the islands' other languages. Spanish influence can be found, however, in the names of many places on the islands—San Rafael, Las Cuevas, Sangre Grande, Los Iros, and many more. Words for types of food and drink have also retained a Spanish flavor, such as *pelau*, *sancoche*, *pastelle*, *sapodilla,* and *granadilla*.

Due to Trinidad's location off the coast of South America, the country has been interested in redeveloping a connection with the region's Spanish-speaking peoples. Historically, people from Venezuela traveled to Trinidad and Tobago to learn English, and the recent arrival of Venezuelan refugees has reinforced the presence of Spanish on the islands. In 2005, the government launched the Spanish as the First Foreign Language (SAFFL) initiative to promote the learning of Spanish above other foreign languages. Many English schools have expanded to feature both English and Spanish. Today, the SAFFL program is part of the Ministry of Education.

## MEDIA OUTLETS

Trinidad has several daily newspapers, the conservative *Trinidad Guardian*, founded in 1917, being the oldest. Another popular read is the *Independent*. Tabloid daily newspapers are very widely read. These news sources are photograph-oriented and full of local gossip. Popular examples are the *Trinidad Express* and *Trinidad and Tobago Newsday*. The *Guardian* also took on a tabloid format in 2002. All of these papers have large weekend versions and are available online.

In Tobago, the single paper is *Tobago News*, published on Fridays, so most Tobagonians read the Trinidad papers. Trinidadians and Tobagonians are also

**Here are some of the newspapers available in Trinidad and Tobago.**

fond of foreign magazines, which are readily available in the cities. Trinidad produces magazines for its own population as well, such as *Sweet TnT Magazine*, an online magazine focused on the positive culture of Trinidad and Tobago, and *Paradise Pulse*, an online lifestyle magazine.

Television is not as widely available in Trinidad and Tobago as it is in the United States. There are 6 free-to-air TV networks and 24 subscription providers, some of which broadcast on cable and others on satellite services. There are commercial broadcasting networks, such as CNC3, which broadcasts news, primetime shows, and sporting events. Popular programs include American soap operas such as *The Bold and the Beautiful*, situation comedies, American game shows, and lots of music programs that focus on local music and musicians, particularly late at night when there are live broadcasts. Most TV owners also have access to cable TV, which allows many American channels such as CNN, Discovery, and HBO to be broadcast directly into the home. American television programs are also available via satellite, and some streaming networks are available through the internet.

Internet use is becoming more popular as the digital age advances. As of 2019, nearly 80 percent of people in Trinidad and Tobago were using the internet. Many people were also accessing the web via smartphones.

Radio is popular too. Popular radio programs cater to local taste with talk shows and news about big parties and upcoming fetes. Music stations broadcast almost nonstop calypso between November and February before an annual calypso competition, after which the airwaves resound with the music of reggae. There are about 36 Trinidad-based radio stations—a few of them dedicated to Indian movie music and Indian reggae, many to popular music and talk, and several to soca, reggae, and urban music. There are only two major radio stations based out of Tobago.

## INTERNET LINKS

**https://www.studycountry.com/guide/TT-language.htm**
This website offers insight into the various languages spoken in Trinidad and Tobago and their origins.

**https://www.worldatlas.com/articles/what-languages-are-spoken -in-trinidad-and-tobago.html**
This article discusses the myriad of languages spoken in Trinidad and Tobago.

ARTS

A steel band performs at Queen's Park Savannah in Port of Spain, Trinidad, in 2013.

## 10

THERE ARE MANY EXAMPLES OF ART that have emerged out of the rich culture of Trinidad and Tobago. Many have been embraced by the world, such as music, literature, dance, and visual arts. Out of all of them, however, music has been the most influential in reaching a mass audience. Through this artistic medium, Trinidadians and Tobagonians have connected in a way that allows them to express themselves and the facets of their roots and heritage. Other forms of art help preserve the history of the people of Trinidad and Tobago as well, and many of these can be viewed in art galleries and museums.

"Every culture is unique, but Trinidad is doubly special because of the number of arts and cultural traditions that have been preserved and cross-pollinated by generations of migrants from all over the world, all in one small island." —Discover Trinidad & Tobago website

## STEEL BANDS

The origins of the steel band in Trinidad and Tobago extend as far back as the 19th century, when neo-African and East Indian drum ensembles came together to play for street and religious ceremonial processions.

The 1884 Peace Preservation Ordinance prohibited the playing of drums, stick-fighting (*calinda*), and the brandishing of burning cane (*canboulay*). In protest of this law, large groups of Carnival masqueraders were organized, and they would sing in tents and in the streets of Trinidad and Tobago.

In the 1930s and 1940s, steel bands began to be used in masked processions and parades during Carnival.

The steel band is one of the country's most distinctive contributions to world music, and it reflects the talent of ordinary people who may not be able to read musical notes but who are nonetheless able to play an astonishing variety of different types of music. This variety extends from internationally recognized classical pieces by composers like Mozart to contemporary music written for and by working-class musicians who seek to comment on social and political life.

The steel drum, more commonly known as the pan or steelpan, is the defining instrument of the steel band. In the 1940s, at the end of World War II, huge oil drums, or metal barrels, littered the islands. These oil drums started being used instead of dustbins, pots, garbage can lids, and other materials that had been used by musicians who were too poor to afford standard percussion instruments. Soon, changes were made to these oil drums, making them more elaborate and better tuned so they could produce different musical notes. There started to be more competition between rival steel bands, and this encouraged experimentation of pan design and tuning. In 1963, the competition Panorama was created to allow steelpan musicians to compete against each other in a structured environment. It still occurs today, with competitors going up against each other for large amounts of prize money. The finals are held the weekend before Carnival each year. It was not until the 1980s, though, that the steel band sound entered into the mainstream music market.

## ISLAND MUSIC

Two popular types of music that were born out of Trinidad and Tobago are calypso and soca. Calypso music is more focused on including subtle social commentary regarding themes such as racism and the cost of living, whereas soca music is less serious and more party-oriented.

Calypso originated in the early 19th century and was originally called *caïso* or *cariso*. During Carnival celebrations, slaves would sing and improvise witty and satirical lyrics directed toward figures they disliked. Each group was led by popular singers known as *shatwell*. At first, calypso was performed within

Soca artist Bunji Garlin performs at Kaya Fest in Miami, Florida, in 2017.

the call-and-response format. The exaggerated speech patterns sung were paired with a syncopated (or staggered) rhythm in the music, which is joyful and upbeat in nature. Popular instruments played in calypso music include the *shak-shak* (maraca), guitar, *cuatro* (a guitar-like instrument), steel drums, and *tamboo-bamboo* (bamboo poles of all different lengths that are struck on the ground). Calypso did not reach the mainstream music market until the late 1950s. Some famous calypso singers from Trinidad and Tobago have included Attila the Hun, the Mighty Terror, and Calypso Rose.

The form of music dubbed soca, which is more focused on the party aspect of the music rather than on speaking out about social and political issues, was born out of calypso in the 1970s. Calypso music could not compete with the

## A SPARROW AND A ROSE

*One of the figures most closely associated with the rich talent produced by the craze for calypso is Mighty Sparrow. Born on the island of Grenada, he moved to Trinidad as a small child. He first emerged as a musician in the 1950s. Sparrow released his first album, Calypso Carnival 58, in 1958, and he went on to regularly release an album each year through his own recording company until the late 1980s. He has won the Calypso Monarch and Trinidad's Carnival Road March competitions both eight times.*

*Calypso Rose is another renowned calypso singer from Trinidad. At age 13, she started writing calypsos. She wrote her first calypso song, "Glass Thief," after watching a man steal glasses from a woman at a market. This was the first known calypso song speaking about gender inequality. In 1977, she became the first woman to win Trinidad's Carnival Road March competition, with her song "Gimme More Tempo." The next year, she won what was then called the Calypso King competition, performing her song "I Thank Thee." Her win prompted the victor to be renamed Calypso Monarch. Today, she continues entertaining crowds with her music, having put out over 1,000 songs and 20 albums.*

Calypso Rose was the first woman to win Trinidad's Carnival Road March competition and the Calypso King (now Calypso Monarch) contest.

emergence of pop and disco music at the time; however, soca included similar elements and became the new popular genre of the islands. The musician most closely associated with the birth of soca is Lord Shorty, or as he is now known, Ras Shorty I. He sped up the tempo of calypso and made it more compatible with the funky dance music that was sweeping across the United States. The synthesizers and other electronic aids to musical composition that were fueling the disco craze also found a place in the rejuvenated calypso sound. Soca is currently the most popular form of music in Trinidad and Tobago, and it dominates the big festivals, especially Carnival. There is now a well-established annual competition that awards the victor the title of the International Soca Monarch, or ruler. Some popular soca artists include Machel Montano, Destra Garcia, and Bunji Garlin.

Another form of music that evolved out of calypso and soca is chutney soca, which incorporates elements of each and is popular in the Indian community, as it was created with East Indian influence. Chutney soca displays the fast-paced tempo of traditional soca, married to and merging with the sound of sitars and other Indian instruments. Songs feature Hindi and English lyrics. The synthesis is mirrored in the dance movements of chutney soca, which manage to combine the gusto of calypso dancing with the highly formalized hand and arm movements of classical Indian dance.

## HOLIDAY MUSIC

During Christmastime in Trinidad and Tobago, the traditional music played is *parang* (par-ANG), which comes from the Spanish word *parranda*, meaning the action of merrymaking and also referring to a group of serenaders. The exact origins of parang are unclear. There are two theories, one being that this music was brought by the early Spanish colonists, and the other that it was created by Venezuelans brought in to work on the cocoa estates in the 19th century. This kind of music is heard throughout the month of December and into January, and the musicians are known as *parranderos* (par-an-DARE-owes). In the past, it was traditional for parang serenaders to pay nighttime visits to the homes of family and friends, where part of the fun was singing to wake the inhabitants of the household from their beds.

The nickname of the national soccer team of Trinidad and Tobago, the Soca Warriors, refers to the musical genre soca.

While Derek Walcott hailed from Saint Lucia, he became a famous writer after he moved to Trinidad.

## LITERARY HISTORY

Trinidad and Tobago's literary tradition can be traced back to at least the 1930s, when a diverse group of young writers began to experiment with different literary forms. Short stories and poems began to appear in print, and novels made their first debuts soon after.

After World War II, Samuel Selvon, a local East Indian writer, made an impact with his humorous novel *A Brighter Sun*. The novel describes East Indians and Creoles (a person of mixed European and black descent) in Trinidad and their prejudices. Selvon later wrote the gritty novel *The Lonely Londoners*, which is set in London in the postwar era. This story tells the sad reality of the racism often encountered by immigrants coming to Britain from Trinidad and Tobago to start a new life. Equally influential has been the work of the West Indian writer Earl Lovelace, especially his powerful novel *The Dragon Can't Dance*, which explores the phenomenon of Carnival.

Derek Walcott was another esteemed poet and playwright who achieved international renown. In 1962, Walcott published a collection of his poetry, entitled *In a Green Night: Poems 1948—1960*, and like much of his early work, the poems proclaim with affection the natural beauty of the West Indies. Walcott's work examines the predicament of coming from a black culture and yet being influenced by a mainstream European culture. In 1957, he went to New York City to study theater. Two years later, he founded and directed the Trinidad Theater Workshop, and out of this artistic venture emerged a number of talented actors. In 1992, Walcott was awarded the Nobel Prize for Literature, the most prestigious literary award in the world.

V. S. Naipaul, another winner of the Nobel Prize for Literature, was a novelist whose work and influence have made themselves powerfully felt around the world. Naipaul was the son of indentured laborers who immigrated to Trinidad from India. He eventually left Trinidad after he won a scholarship that took him to Oxford University in England, where he studied literature. His first novel was published in the 1950s, but it was the publication of *A House for Mr. Biswas* in 1961 that established his fame as a writer. After traveling through

## LIMBO DANCE

*The exhilarating dance of limbo originated in Trinidad in the mid-to-late 19th century as a ritual performed at wakes. During a limbo, a dancer moves to the rhythm of the music while lowering himself or herself under a horizontal stick or bar, which is held up by a person on each side of the stick or placed on two vertical bars. The goal is to not knock off or touch the stick while going under it. Each time someone knocks the bar or touches it, they are eliminated, and the bar is set to a lower position, making it more challenging for the next contestant.*

*Shemika Campbell, who is a native of Trinidad, moved to Buffalo, New York, when she was 8 years old. After seeing her mother perform limbo, she dreamed of being onstage doing it as well. At 14, she began limbo training for 6 hours a day with her uncle. Campbell is currently a two-time Guinness World Record holder for the lowest limbo by a female, at 8.5 inches (21.6 cm) off the floor, and for limboing the longest distance, traveling a little more than 10 feet, 3 inches (3.12 m) while going under a bar set at 12 inches (30.5 cm). She has appeared on* The Ellen DeGeneres Show, America's Got Talent, *and many other programs to share her unique talent with the world.*

**Shemika Charles shows off her talent as she limbos underneath a pole on fire during a show for Aerial Angels Australia.**

the Caribbean, he published *The Middle Passage* in 1962 and expressed the view that the West Indies as a region was a home to displaced people who did not have their own cultural identity. This point of view, and his exposure of the corrupting effect of colonialism in places like Trinidad, did not always endear him to established figures in his country.

Monique Roffey and Amanda Smyth are two more recent writers who have released works that have achieved international success. Roffey's novel *The White Woman on the Green Bicycle* was shortlisted for the 2010 Orange Prize for fiction, and she won the 2013 Bocas Prize for her novel *Archipelago*. Smyth's first novel, *Black Rock*, won the Prix du Premier Roman Etranger and was shortlisted for a National Association for the Advancement of Colored People (NAACP) Image Award.

The National Museum, which houses some of Trinidad and Tobago's most prestigious art, is located in Port of Spain.

## ART MUSEUMS

The visual arts of Trinidad and Tobago are less celebrated than other forms of art; however, visual art still serves a significant purpose within the country's culture. Some of the most prestigious local art is housed in the seven galleries at the National Museum, which was established in 1892. It was originally called the Royal Victoria Institute, as it was built for Queen Victoria's Jubilee, or 50th year of rule. A highlight of the museum's collection is a set of watercolor paintings done by 19th-century painter Michel-Jean Cazabon, Trinidad's first internationally known artist. In addition, there are depictions of national festivals, such as Carnival, and displays of ancient artifacts from some of the country's earliest settlers, including the Amerindians. Some of the other galleries that host art exhibitions all year round include 101 Art Gallery, Horizons, Medulla, Softbox Studios, and Studio 66.

## INTERNET LINKS

**http://www.bbc.com/culture/story/20171010-the-surprising-politics-of-calypso**
This website discusses the roots of calypso music.

**https://www.discovertnt.com/articles/Trinidad/Trinidad-Arts-Culture-An-Overview/60/3/19#axzz66h2Qjmel**
This website provides information on the arts and cultural scenes in Trinidad and Tobago.

**https://omeka1.grinnell.edu/MusicalInstruments/exhibits/show/ens/steel**
This website discusses the history of steel bands in Trinidad and Tobago.

**https://theculturetrip.com/caribbean/trinidad-tobago/articles/trinidadian-writers-you-should-know**
This website showcases five famous Trinidadian writers.

# LEISURE

People in Scarborough, Tobago, relax
outside a grocery store.

## 11

PLANNING AMPLE TIME FOR LEISURE is a major priority for the people of Trinidad and Tobago. While it is crucial to work and make a living, it is also important to relax and connect with family and friends regularly.

Besides hanging out with their friends, the people of the islands also enjoy many other pursuits. Sports such as cricket, soccer, golf, and water activities are extremely popular, and the beaches and city parks are excellent places for these activities. In addition, technology also affects people's lives, providing entertainment such as soap operas, documentaries, and movies on television, as well as news and music on the radio.

## THE ART OF DOING NOTHING

Liming is a laid-back activity with no particular structure to it that appeals to those living in Trinidad and Tobago. It basically involves relaxing and doing nothing. A typical lime can take place in someone's home or yard, on the beach, on the street, or at a calypso performance. In many cultures, people hanging around doing nothing is seen as shameful or lazy; in Trinidad and Tobago, however, this behavior is celebrated. People from all different social classes participate in liming.

When someone leaves a liming session when it is going really well, otherwise known as "breaking a lime," this is seen as a bad social gaffe, or problem. When someone does this, it reminds all the other limers that they also may have something to do and that they also should leave. This

"Trinidad & Tobago is part of the Caribbean, and therefore has that laid-back vibe and carefree way of thinking present in many island cultures. Here, however, they take doing nothing to another level."

—Jessica Festa, blogger

Duane O'Connor Jr. has won the Junior Calypso Monarch competition.

can be bad for a party, and so the accusation of breaking a lime is a particularly bad one.

## THE LATEST CALYPSO

Calypso is not only a musical genre enjoyed by those in Trinidad and Tobago, but it is also a way of life. Many people listen to calypso every day on the radio. Within the lyrics, there are powerful messages regarding social and political issues. People spend much of their leisure time discussing the latest calypso songs and analyzing the lyrics. Those who are unfamiliar with the political scene may not be able to participate in the conversation due to their lack of knowledge on the topic. Calypso is known as the poor people's newspaper, and songs often say in an obscure way things that would lead to legal actions if they were said by a politician or another person in a place of power.

Every year in Trinidad, there are two major calypso competitions: the Calypso Monarch and Carnival Road March. Long before an event begins, calypso players set up huge tents to practice. Anyone can join the players in their tents and listen to their music.

## FETES AND CONCERTS

When the calypso season is over, young people like to spend the summer listening to reggae and rapso music. Reggae is a style of music that originated in Jamaica in the late 1960s. It features a heavy four-beat rhythm created by drums, bass guitar, electric guitar, and the "scraper," which is a corrugated stick that is rubbed by a plain stick. Rapso is the local form of reggae. It originated in Trinidad and Tobago in the 1970s and involves African drumbeats and spoken lyrics, often of a political nature. Both music genres are played widely on the radio, but there are also large open-air concerts where a variety of reggae and rapso artists perform. The concert might take place in a city park, with a DJ playing lots of music from Jamaica as well as local bands performing live.

Young people will happily spend the night and early hours dancing to local bands. These big parties or concerts are known locally as fetes.

Nightclubs are also very popular after work and especially on the weekends. They open late, at about 10:00 p.m., and their closing time is generally "till," which means they are open till the last person has gone home. Nightclubs are typically more sophisticated and expensive than fetes.

Audience members enjoy the Machel Monday Journey of a Soca King concert at Hasely Crawford Stadium during Carnival in 2017.

## SHOPS AND MARKETS

Shopping at malls and markets in Trinidad is another leisurely activity residents and tourists enjoy. Most of the shopping malls carry American and European designer clothes. In the 1970s, during the oil boom, there was a general feeling of wealth, and many people flew to the United States during the weekend to go

*Hasely Crawford was born in San Fernando in 1950. He began pursuing track and field at the age of 17. His first big race was in 1970 at the Commonwealth Games, where he took home the bronze medal for the 100-meter race. At the 1976 Montreal Olympics, Crawford finished the 100-meter final race in 10.06 seconds, winning the first gold medal for his country. He also competed in three other Olympic Games.*

*Ato Boldon was born in Port of Spain in 1973. Boldon started out playing soccer and transitioned to track and field at the age of 16. At 18, he represented his country in the 100-meter and 200-meter sprints at the 1992 Barcelona Olympics. However, he did not qualify in the first round of either event. That didn't stop him, though. At the 1996 Olympics in Atlanta, Georgia, he won bronze medals in the 100- and 200-meter sprints. Then, in the 2000 Sydney Olympics, he took home the silver medal in the 100-meter sprint and bronze medal in the 200-meter sprint.*

Track star Hasely Crawford is shown here at the 1984 Summer Olympics in Los Angeles, California.

shopping. Recently, the struggling economic climate has reduced this activity. However, Trinidadians love to shop, even if only to look at the goods being offered. Shopping extends also to the little stores and stalls on the streets, such as in marketplaces, and a great deal of liming can take place during a shopping trip when friends meet outside a store or on the street.

## SPECTATOR SPORTS

The most popular sport played in Trinidad and Tobago is cricket. Most parks have several cricket fields, called pitches, and small cricket matches are played on the streets by children. Cricket is a game that is most common in the British Commonwealth countries (nations once belonging to the British Empire), and its rules are very complex. Some cricket matches, called tests, can last up to five days, with six hours of playing time each day. In Trinidad and Tobago, most professional matches take place in March and April in Port of Spain. The events include loud soca music, lots of cold drinks, and excited cheering when someone begins a series of runs. Much liming goes on at cricket matches.

The second most popular sport is football, otherwise known as soccer. When children are not playing cricket in the street, they are generally playing soccer.

Additional sporting activities involve water sports such as sailing, surfing, windsurfing, scuba diving, and swimming around the reefs off Tobago; however, swimming off the shore can be quite dangerous. The waters sometimes have sharks and jellyfish swimming in them, and strong currents can drag

The Trinidad and Tobago national soccer team poses for a photograph before playing a match in 2019.

unsuspecting swimmers underneath the waves. There are windsurfing competitions in the islands each year.

Golf is another sport played on the islands; however, most people who play golf belong to an exclusive golf club. There are several golf courses in Trinidad and two in Tobago, all privately owned. There are no public golf courses.

## SCOUTING ADVENTURES

Most children in Trinidad and Tobago attend religious services at a church, temple, or mosque, and a large part of their weekends is taken up with religious activities. Another activity for young people is scouting, or learning survival and safety skills in the wild. In 1911, the Scout Movement was introduced to the country from the United Kingdom. Trinidad and Tobago became a member of the World Organization of the Scout Movement in 1963. The Scout Movement in Trinidad and Tobago has a strong following. Scouts wear a special uniform, and their activities involve hiking in the countryside, camping, and practicing scouting skills such as flower identification, first aid, survival, swimming, and safety. Scout groups meet once a week in the evenings and study for a series of badges in each skill.

## PARK ACTIVITIES

The largest open recreational space in Trinidad is the Queen's Park Savannah in Port of Spain, which is simply called "the Savannah" by locals. Various leisure activities are often carried out in this huge park, which was established in the middle of the 19th century. Many people say the park is like an enormous traffic circle in the middle of the city, and that all traffic weaves its way around it. The park has a perimeter of 2.2 miles (3.5 km) and spans 260 acres (105 ha). During the hot working hours, the park is relatively empty, but after about 4:00 p.m., it comes alive with plenty of activities. Part of the park is divided into soccer fields, and they are constantly full of players. Other areas are dedicated to cricket. Runners do circuits of the many paths around the park.

At the southern end of the park is the old racetrack, which used to feature horse races and is now called the Grand Stand. The races have since moved to

Arima, but the former grounds are home to all the biggest festivals in town, such as Carnival, and many smaller fetes. The streets outside the park are lined with vans and trucks selling tasty food.

On the western side of the Savannah are the Magnificent Seven Houses, which are old Victorian buildings. These buildings include residences of the Anglican bishop and the Roman Catholic archbishop, Queen's Royal College, and the prime minister's office.

This is one of the Magnificent Seven Houses, a group of mansions on the western side of the Queen's Park Savannah.

## INTERNET LINKS

**http://www.bestoftrinidad.com/cricket.html**
This website provides information on the sport of cricket in Trinidad and Tobago.

**https://www.destinationtnt.com/queens-park-savannah**
This website gives a description of Queen's Park Savannah and all the sights it has to offer.

**https://epicureandculture.com/what-is-liming**
This website describes what "liming" is and its significance to people in Trinidad and Tobago.

# FESTIVALS

Carnival is the biggest and most popular annual festival in Trinidad and Tobago.

## 12

THERE ARE FESTIVALS CELEBRATED by all the different cultural groups in Trinidad and Tobago. While these celebrations may have been started or recognized by a specific group, now Trinidadians and Tobagonians come together as a whole to honor these special occasions. Celebrating a festival is not restricted to any one group or religion. The country's pleasant climate and the disposition of its people encourage residents and visitors alike to join in on whatever festivities may be happening.

In total, there are 14 official public holidays where all the workplaces close, shops have special sales, and special events and concerts are held to mark the event. Drawing from Islam, Hinduism, and various branches of Christianity, the public holidays reflect the islands' cultural diversity.

## THE MAGIC OF CARNIVAL

Carnival is the biggest festival of the year in Trinidad and Tobago. It originated in the late 18th century, when French settlers brought the Fat Tuesday (Mardi Gras) masquerade party tradition to the islands. This celebration, which takes place in February or March each year on the

*Some say Carnival comes from the Roman festival Saturnalia, a lively celebration honoring the god Saturn. Saturnalia was held in December and marked the winter planting season. By the Middle Ages, it had become the Feast of Fools, a French celebration of the New Year that came before the 40 days of fasting and denial of Lent. The event was always an outrageous affair, frowned on by the Catholic Church. Because of its place on the calendar, some also associate the ancient Saturnalia festival with the modern celebration of Christmas.*

Monday and Tuesday before the first day of Lent, eventually spread to the rest of the Caribbean.

Originally, the festival was a serious religious affair, with great dances, called balls, where French planters, who were the elite at the time, wore fancy clothes and masks, drank wine, and impressed their neighbors. While the elite enjoyed themselves, slaves out in the yard had their own party. Once the slaves were freed, they continued their celebration, naming it Canboulay. This celebration gradually overtook that of the elites and is considered the precursor to today's Carnival celebrations in the country.

Over time, African elements entered the Carnival processions, which spilled into the streets with drumming, costumes, and lots of noise. Originally, Carnival spanned three days before Ash Wednesday (the start of Lent), but today it consists of just one day—Tuesday. The festival was moved from three days to one because of the rowdy nature it created among the celebrators. People would take to the streets in droves, drumming, fighting with sticks, and masquerading. At one point, these festivities were banned. Chaos sometimes ensued. In 1881, for instance, British soldiers were ordered to calm down the procession, but they ended up triggering protests instead. These became known as the Canboulay Riots.

As the years went on, Carnival became a bit more subdued but was never officially put to rest. In the 1890s, a series of competitions were encouraged by the government to help clean up the event. First there was a band competition, then a calypso competition, a costume competition, and others. In the 1940s, the modern steel band emerged. During World War II, Carnival was banned, but by the 1950s, the festival came back with the Calypso King (now called Calypso Monarch) competition, and it has never looked back.

## HOSAY FESTIVAL

**The sun sets during the Hosay Festival in Saint James, Trinidad.**

Hosay is a festival celebrated by Trinidadians from all different backgrounds; however, traditionally it has roots in the Muslim portion of the country's East Indian community. The festival, observed by Shia Muslims, was first celebrated in Trinidad in 1847 in San Fernando. In the beginning, it was recognized as a sad and solemn affair commemorating the martyrdom, or religious death, of Husayn, a grandson of Muhammad, the Prophet of Islam, in 680 CE. The event also commemorates Husayn's brother, Hassan, who died several years earlier. However, over time it developed into a joyous and noisy occasion. In the past, wailing women walked through the streets crying out behind replicas of the tombs of the martyrs. Now, fire-eaters, Indian drummers, and whirling dancers entertain crowds in the streets.

The festival runs for four days. It is scheduled according to the Islamic lunar calendar and can therefore fall at any time of year. Before the true festivities begin, there are six days of fasting, prayer meetings, and the constructing of large and small *tadjahs*, which are models of mosques said to represent the tombs of Husayn and Hassan. On the first day of the festival, multicolored flags are paraded around the town. This represents the Battle of Karbala, in which Husayn was killed, and is called Flag Night. For the second day, a procession is held, led by the elaborate tadjahs representing the martyrs' tombs. The procession includes dancers and drumming. On the third day, smaller tadjahs are paraded around the town. This is also known as the dance of the moon, since two huge moons, representing the martyrs themselves, are danced through the streets by special performers. At midnight, the two moons are brought into contact to symbolize the two martyr brothers' triumph over death. All this is done to the rhythm of Indian tassa drums. Dancers perform a stick dance playing out a mock battle with stick and shield. On the fourth and final day, the moons and tombs are taken to the sea, where they are cast into the water after prayers.

January 1 . . . . . . . . . . New Year's Day
March 30 . . . . . . . . . Spiritual Baptist/Shouter Liberation Day
April 10 . . . . . . . . . . Good Friday
April 12–April 13 . . . . . Easter Sunday/Easter Monday
May 23–24 . . . . . . . . Eid al-Fitr
May 30 . . . . . . . . . . Indian Arrival Day
June 11 . . . . . . . . . . Corpus Christi
June 19 . . . . . . . . . . Labour Day
August 1 . . . . . . . . . Emancipation Day (of Trinidad and Tobago)
August 31 . . . . . . . . Independence Day
September 24 . . . . . . . Trinidad and Tobago Republic Day
November 14 . . . . . . . Diwali (main day of celebrating)
December 25 . . . . . . . Christmas Day
December 26 . . . . . . . Boxing Day

## DIWALI FESTIVAL

Diwali, the Hindu Festival of Lights, is held for five days each year. These days change every year, but they usually fall somewhere in late October and November. This is a major religious festival that honors Lakshmi, the goddess of light, wealth, and beauty, and celebrates the triumph of good over evil. In the weeks before the event, Diwali queens, or mock royalty, are chosen in an event similar to a modern beauty pageant. There are also concerts and musical competitions. On the night before, little oil lamps known as *deyas* are lit all over houses and in the streets to light the goddess's way. In towns that celebrate the event, the small lamps are supported by strings of colored electric lights. Fireworks are also a part of the occasion, which is fun even for non-Hindus. For Diwali, people exchange gifts, and there is feasting in every house that celebrates this occasion.

Dancers perform during the Diwali celebration in Chaguanas, Trinidad.

## CELEBRATING EID AL-FITR

The festival of Eid al-Fitr marks the end of Ramadan, which is the Muslim month of fasting from dawn till dusk. Eid al-Fitr is Arabic for "festival of the breaking of the fast." Each year, the imams decide the day long in advance. The date varies from year to year because it is determined by the lunar calendar, which means it may fall in any season of the year. On the day itself, there is a visit to the mosque, and donations are given to the poor. Everyone wears new clothes, and houses are thoroughly cleaned. There are official dinners during which people from other religions attend, and the traditional dish *sawine* (SAY-wine) is served. This is prepared with vermicelli (a thin pasta) boiled in milk with raisins, sugar, and chopped almonds. In private homes, the family gathers for a similar celebration of the end of Ramadan and a sense of renewal and spiritual cleanliness. Unlike other celebrations, this one has not given way to the usual wild partying and remains a quiet family affair.

An issue over the years has been Trinidad and Tobago's lack of special celebrations for Chinese citizens. However, the annual Dragon Boat Festival is one of the main Chinese events that commemorates the arrival of the first Chinese people on the islands.

## INTERNET LINKS

**https://www.destinationtnt.com/blog/a-land-of-endless-festivals**
This website mentions 20 must-see festivals in Trinidad and Tobago.

**https://www.discovertnt.com/articles/Trinidad/The-Birth
-Evolution-of-Trinidad-Carnival/109/3/32#axzz64z9FyVPx**
This website discusses the birth and evolution of Carnival.

**http://www.tntisland.com/festivals.html**
This website lists all of Trinidad and Tobago's holidays.

# FOOD

Callaloo is a Caribbean soup-like dish made of vegetables, seasonings, spices, and seafood.

**13**

THERE IS NO ONE NATIONAL DISH that represents Trinidad and Tobago because of how diversified the people and the cultures of the islands are. This melting pot of cultures has allowed for the introduction of a variety of foods of different tastes and styles. Many of these tastes and styles have been blended to make special fusion cuisines.

The people of Trinidad and Tobago love food because it is a part of enjoying life and socializing with others. There is always a reason to prepare something tasty to eat, and offering food to a guest is part of the island's etiquette.

## CREOLE CUISINE

When the term "creole" is applied to food in Trinidad and Tobago, it refers to those dishes and styles of cooking that have their origins in Africa. Over time, European culture has also immersed itself within this cuisine. Creole cooking has thus become a mixture of different influences and their interpretations of African cuisine.

*Pelau* (PEL-ow) is a typical and highly popular creole dish that uses chicken, savory pigeon peas, and other vegetables, along with garlic, peppers, and onions. The ingredients are cooked in coconut milk and served with rice. What gives pelau its appealing taste is the mixture of spices that are added. Although the types and exact balance of spices is up to the cook, cinnamon is sometimes part of the mixture.

Another creole dish made in Trinidad and Tobago is callaloo, which is like a stew with the consistency of soup. This dish may include okra, greens, coconut milk, crab, conch, Caribbean lobster, pumpkin, chili peppers, and additional seasonings. It is regularly eaten with macaroni pie.

## INDIAN CUISINE

Indian food, alongside creole cooking, is a popular part of the national cuisine. Although its origins and its vocabulary come from India, most of the dishes found in Trinidad and Tobago have a Caribbean taste that would not be instantly recognized by someone in India.

The Indian bread roti is found everywhere in Trinidad and Tobago. It is affordable and is enjoyed at all times of the day or night. The roti is stretchable,

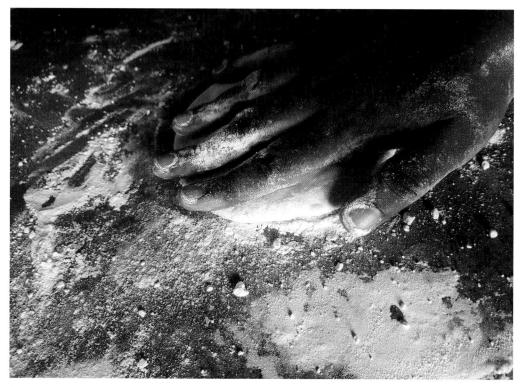

A Caribbean cook is shown here kneading roti.

and this makes it ideal for filling with curried meats, fish, and vegetables. There are different types of roti, but the most common kind is called *dhalpuri* (dal-POUR-ee). This is easily and quickly made using two layers of dough to form a thin sandwich of split peas. This tasty sandwich can then be stuffed with whatever other ingredients the cook chooses, such as the usual curried beef, chicken, and shrimp; however, a more daring cook might throw in pieces of shark meat, pumpkin, or spinach.

## BEVERAGES AND DESSERTS

The national alcoholic drink of Trinidad and Tobago is rum. Some of it is exported, although Trinidadian rum has not achieved the same degree of international recognition as that produced in Jamaica and Barbados.

This is *mauby*, which is made with the extract of the bark of the mauby tree.

Another well-known alcohol from Trinidad is Angostura bitters, or simply "bitters." Developed in Venezuela by Dr. Johann Siegert in 1824, Angostura bitters was originally conceived of as a medicine but is more typically used in small quantities to add flavor to other alcoholic drinks. The Angostura bitters buisness was brought over to Trinidad by Siegert's sons in 1875, and manufacturing then took off. Today, the company, House of Angostura, still exists, and several varieties of the drink have been made. It remains headquartered in Trinidad and Tobago.

There are plenty of nonalcoholic beverages available on the islands as well. One popular drink is made from the petals of the sorrel flower, and another, called *mauby* (MAO-by), is an extract from the bark of the mauby tree. The sea provides another nutritional drink in the form of sea moss, which is liquified and mixed with milk.

Trinidad and Tobago is blessed with a rich variety of edible fruits, such as mangoes, guavas, and bananas. Many fruits are used to produce fruit juices and punch, which is what Americans would call a smoothie. Coconut juice (or water) is sold everywhere by mobile street vendors. These vendors use their long

Coconut jelly is a jello-like dish made using coconut meat, gelatin, coconut milk, and cow's milk. It's sometimes served in a coconut shell.

curved knives, called machetes, to split open the coconuts. They can tell if the coconuts are ripe for opening by shaking the fruit.

On hot days, locals enjoy a variety of cold desserts, including ice cream, snow cones (served in many different colors, flavors, and shapes, often with sweetened condensed milk), ice pops, and coconut slushies, as well as fresh coconut jelly.

## FOOD INSECURITY

Over the years, there has been concern that Caribbean countries within CARICOM have less food security than other countries around the world. In Trinidad and Tobago, as in several other CARICOM member nations, more than 80 percent of food is imported. This means food production within the country is declining, and there is less access to safe and nutritious food. Having to rely on outside countries for food is not the best option for the people of Trinidad and Tobago. While some feel it is vital for the country to introduce a more stable food security program, Prime Minister Keith Rowley downplayed the issue in 2018, saying, "There is not enough land." He added, "Agriculture will never be as commercially viable to the T&T [Trinidad and Tobago] economy as oil and gas because the country does not have the land space to be a global player in the field."

For years, the Ministry of Agriculture in Trinidad and Tobago has attempted to launch a National Food Security Program in which 25 percent of all food consumed would be domestically produced. However, the prices of locally produced food are much more expensive than cheaper imports, which does not give the islands' people much incentive to buy local. The government has considered many ways to increase the amount of agricultural land, including leasing state land to prospective farmers and implementing more urban and kitchen gardens for food production.

Between 2011 and 2016, 7.4 percent of people in Trinidad and Tobago were undernourished.

## SEAFOOD

Trinidad and Tobago is known for the bounty of seafood available, especially in major cities, such as Port of Spain. Seafood can be purchased from local merchants and in marketplaces. Some of the popular seafood available includes flying fish, kingfish, squid, shrimp, lobster, mussels, conch, and crab.

Seafood, such as crab, is popular on the islands of Trinidad and Tobago.

Many of the seafood dishes made are curried, stewed, or barbecued. Some examples of dishes are curried crab and dumplings, fish broth, and Trinidad stew fry fish. Another popular seafood street food is called bake and shark, which is a fish sandwich made with a thick piece of deep-fried shark meat put in between two pieces of fried bread. There is also the seasonal *cascadu*, or cascadura, which is a fish found in freshwater swamps during the country's dry season. Cascadura is normally curried and served with rice, cassava, and yams.

Trinidad and Tobago has a lot to offer its residents and visitors when it comes to food, culture, people, wildlife, and other unique experiences. The variety of different cultures there makes it a place full of diversity and endless options to try new things and have fun adventures.

## INTERNET LINKS

**https://www.simplycaribbean.net/?v=7516fd43adaa**
Many delicious Caribbean food recipes are posted on this website.

**https://www.simplytrinicooking.com**
This blog includes some of Trinidad's most popular recipes.

There is a local legend in Trinidad that claims whoever eats cascadu will stay in Trinidad for the rest of their life.

# CHICKEN *PELAU* (CARIBBEAN STEW)

*6 servings*

3 tablespoons brown sugar
1 pound of chicken, cut in 1-inch pieces
1½ cups water
1 cup coconut milk
½ cup uncooked brown rice
2 cups fresh pigeon peas
1 cup chopped carrot
3 tablespoons coarsely chopped
  fresh parsley

Cook brown sugar in a large saucepan over medium heat until it begins to caramelize.

Stir in the chicken, and cook until well browned.

Add the water, coconut milk, rice, pigeon peas, and carrot to the mix, and bring to a simmer.

Cover and cook until rice is done, about 25 minutes.

Stir in parsley to garnish.

# CASSAVA PONE

*8 servings*

3 cups cassava
1 cup pumpkin
½ cup coconut milk
1 cup brown sugar
½ teaspoon ground nutmeg
1 teaspoon ground cinnamon
1 teaspoon vanilla extract
2 tablespoons melted butter
1 cup evaporated milk
1 cup desiccated (dried) coconut
1 teaspoon grated fresh ginger
1 teaspoon baking powder
½ cup raisins

Peel, wash, and grate the cassava and pumpkin.

In a large bowl, combine coconut milk, brown sugar, ground nutmeg, ground cinnamon, and vanilla extract.

Whisk well to break down the sugar.

Add the cassava, pumpkin, butter, evaporated milk, desiccated (dried) coconut, fresh ginger, baking powder, and raisins, and mix well.

Meanwhile, preheat oven to 350°F (175°C), and grease a baking dish.

Pour the batter into the greased baking dish, and place on the middle rack of your hot oven. Bake for 1 hour.

Stick a toothpick into the middle of the pone. If it comes out clean, it means it's fully cooked.

Allow it to cool before slicing.

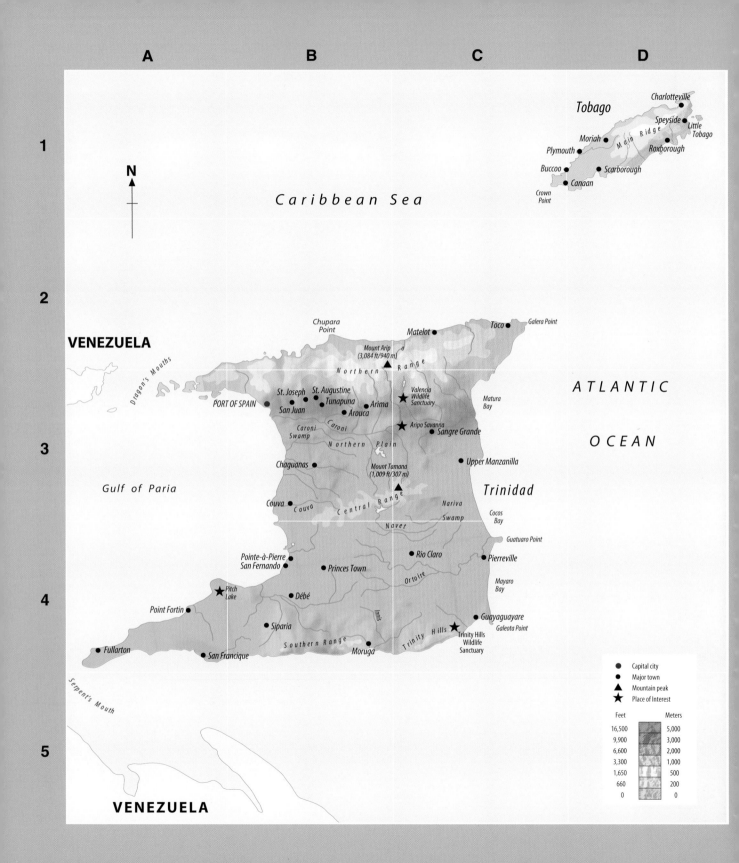

**A**   **B**   **C**   **D**

**1**

**2**

**3**

**4**

**5**

N

*Caribbean Sea*

*Tobago*

Charlotteville
Speyside
*Main Ridge*
Little Tobago
Moriah
Plymouth
Roxborough
Buccoo
Scarborough
Canaan
Crown Point

VENEZUELA

*Dragon's Mouths*

Chupara Point

Matelot
Toco
Galera Point

Mount Arip (3,084 ft/940 m)

*Northern Range*

St. Joseph
St. Augustine
Tunapuna
Arima
PORT OF SPAIN
San Juan
Arouca

Valencia Wildlife Sanctuary

*Matura Bay*

*ATLANTIC*

*Caroni Swamp*

*Caroni*

*Northern Plain*

Aripo Savanna
Sangre Grande

*OCEAN*

Chaguanas

Mount Tamana (1,009 ft/307 m)

Upper Manzanilla

*Trinidad*

*Gulf of Paria*

Couva
*Couva*
*Central Range*

*Nariva Swamp*

*Navet*

*Cocos Bay*

Guataro Point

Pointe-à-Pierre
San Fernando

Rio Claro
Pierreville

*Ortoire*
*Mayaro Bay*

Princes Town

Pitch Lake

Point Fortin

Débé

*Innis*

Guayaguayare
Galeota Point

Siparia

Trinity Hills Wildlife Sanctuary

*Trinity Hills*

Fullarton

San Francique

*Southern Range*

Moruga

*Serpent's Mouth*

VENEZUELA

● Capital city
● Major town
▲ Mountain peak
★ Place of Interest

| Feet | Meters |
|---|---|
| 16,500 | 5,000 |
| 9,900 | 3,000 |
| 6,600 | 2,000 |
| 3,300 | 1,000 |
| 1,650 | 500 |
| 660 | 200 |
| 0 | 0 |

Arima, B3
Aripo Savanna, C3
Arouca, B3
Atlantic Ocean, C1—C5, D1—D5

Buccoo, C1, D1

Canaan, C1, D1
Caribbean Sea, B1—B2, C1—C2
Caroni River, B3
Caroni Swamp, B3
Central Range, B3—B4, C3
Chaguanas, B3
Charlotteville, D1
Chupara Point, B2
Cocos Bay, C3—C4
Couva, B3
Couva River, B3
Crown Point, C1

Débé, B4

Dragon's Mouths, A2—A3

Fullarton, A4

Galeota Point, C4
Galera Point, C2—C3
Guatuaro Point, C4
Guayaguayare, C4
Gulf of Paria, A3

Innis River, B4

Little Tobago, D1

Main Ridge, D1
Matelot, C2
Matura Bay, C3
Mayaro Bay, C4
Moriah, D1
Moruga, B4
Mount Aripo, B2
Mount Tamana, C3

Nariva Swamp, C3
Navet River, B4, C4
Northern Plain, B3, C3
Northern Range, B2, C2

Ortoire River, C4

Pierreville, C4
Pitch Lake, A4
Plymouth, D1
Pointe-à-Pierre, B4
Point Fortin, A4
Port of Spain, B3
Princes Town, B4

Rio Claro, C4
Roxborough, D1

Saint Augustine, B3
Saint Joseph, B3
San Fernando, B4

San Francique, A4
Sangre Grande, C3
San Juan, B3
Scarborough, D1
Serpent's Mouth, A5
Siparia, B4
Southern Range, B4
Speyside, D1

Toco, C2
Trinity Hills, C4
Tunapuna, B3

Upper Manzanilla, C3

Valencia Wildlife Sanctuary, C3
Venezuela, A2—A3, A5, B5

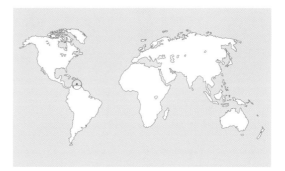

# ECONOMIC TRINIDAD AND TOBAGO

## Natural Resources

 Asphalt

 Natural gas

Petroleum

## Agriculture

Citrus

Cocoa

Coffee

Rice

Vegetables

## Services

 Airport

Port

Tourism

# ABOUT THE ECONOMY

*All figures are 2019 estimates unless otherwise noted.*

## OVERVIEW

The twin-island nation of Trinidad and Tobago experienced a period of negative GDP performance in the middle of the 2010s. In 2019, the country bounced back after small GDP growth in 2018. Long-term growth prospects remain promising, as Trinidad and Tobago further develops its natural gas resources and the industries dependent on natural gas, including petrochemicals and fertilizers. Additional growth potential exists in financial services, telecommunications, and transportation. Trinidad and Tobago has made a transition from an oil-based economy to one based on natural gas. The petrochemical sector includes plants that produce methanol and ammonia. The government is also seeking to diversify the economy to reduce dependence on the energy sector and to achieve self-sustaining growth.

## GROSS DOMESTIC PRODUCT (GDP)

$22.1 billion (2017 estimate)

## CURRENCY

Trinidad and Tobago dollar (TT$)
$1 US = TT $6.76 (2020 estimate)

## LABOR FORCE

669,000

## LABOR FORCE BY FIELD OF WORK

agriculture: 3 percent
industry: 27 percent
services: 70 percent

## UNEMPLOYMENT RATE

2.8 percent

## NATURAL RESOURCES

petroleum, natural gas, asphalt

## AGRICULTURAL PRODUCTS

cocoa, dasheen, pumpkin, cassava, tomato, cucumber, eggplant, hot pepper, pommecythere, coconut water, poultry

## MAIN INDUSTRIES

petroleum and petroleum products, liquefied natural gas, methanol, ammonia, urea, steel products, beverages, food processing, cement, cotton textiles

## MAIN EXPORTS

liquified natural gas, petroleum and petroleum products, methanol, ammonia, urea, steel products, beverages, cereal and cereal products, cocoa, fish, preserved fruits, cosmetics, household cleaners, plastic packaging

## MAIN IMPORTS

mineral fuels, lubricants, machinery, transportation equipment, manufactured goods, food, chemicals, live animals

# CULTURAL TRINIDAD AND TOBAGO

## National Museum and Art Gallery, Port of Spain

The local flavor of the museum is conveyed by an extensive display on the evolution of the pans, masks, and costumes used during Carnival. Industrial histories covered include sugar, cocoa, and coconut agriculture. Two smaller branch museums are Fort San Andres and the Trinidad and Tobago Police Service Museum, located nearby.

## Little Tobago Island

Little Tobago Island on the extreme east end of Tobago, across from Speyside, is an uninhabited bird sanctuary with several miles of trails. Its most spectacular views are from the hills overlooking the seaward direction. Regularly scheduled glass-bottomed boats ferry visitors to the island, revealing the coral reefs below.

## Mount Saint Benedict Monastery

The church tower sitting on the Northern Range Hills above Tunapuna is one of the most striking landmarks east of Port of Spain. This Benedictine monastic community is the largest and oldest in the Caribbean. It was established in 1912 by monks fleeing Brazil's attempt to take over their land.

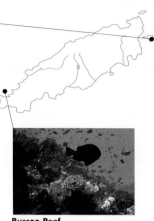

## Buccoo Reef

Tobago's fringing coral reefs are some of the best in the region, and because of its nutrient-rich coastal waters, they are also home to an impressive abundance of marine life, ranging from the microscopic to the huge. Large marine animals frequently seen are sea turtles, reef sharks, hammerhead sharks, groupers, eagle rays, and manta rays.

## Asa Wright Nature Center

This is located in an unspoiled rain forest–covered range of mountains that runs from west to east across the top of Trinidad. The bird species found at the site and that come to the feeders off the veranda are some of the most colorful in Trinidad.

## Caroni Swamp and Bird Sanctuary

This sanctuary is a series of mangrove-lined waterways and lakes, the nesting location of the stunning scarlet ibis, a national bird of Trinidad and Tobago. There are also little herons, egrets, and cormorants. Viewing of the birds is done when one cruises up and down the waterways.

## Nariva Swamp

The Nariva Swamp is the largest freshwater wetland in Trinidad and Tobago and has been designated a Wetland of International Importance under the Ramsar Convention. The area provides an important habitat for waterfowl and is a key habitat for numerous species, including the West Indian manatee.

## Pointe-à-Pierre Wildfowl Trust

This is one of the best bird viewing spots in Trinidad. This 79-acre (32 ha) site is partly for wild birds and partly for breeding cages for endangered species.

## La Brea Pitch Lake

On the southwest tip of Trinidad is one of the world's few open pitch lakes from which this ingredient of asphalt has been mined and exported since 1859. Visitors to the site walk across the fairly solid surface of the lake.

# ABOUT THE CULTURE

*All figures are 2018 estimates unless otherwise noted.*

**OFFICIAL NAME**
Republic of Trinidad and Tobago

**LAND AREA**
1,980 square miles (5,128 sq km)

**CAPITAL**
Port of Spain

**MAJOR PORTS**
Pointe-à-Pierre, Point Fortin, Point Lisas, Port of Spain, Scarborough

**CLIMATE**
tropical: dry season (January—May), wet season (June—December)

**HIGHEST POINT**
Mount Aripo (3,084 feet/940 m)

**COASTLINE**
225 miles (362 km)

**POPULATION**
1,363,985 (2019 estimate)

**AGE STRUCTURE**
0—14 years: 19.2 percent
15—24 years: 11.6 percent
22—54 years: 45 percent
55—64 years: 13.1 percent
65 years and over: 11.1 percent

**BIRTH RATE**
12.3 births per 1,000 population

**ETHNIC GROUPS**
East Indian 35.4 percent, African 34.2 percent, mixed African/East Indian 7.7 percent, other mixed 15.3 percent, other 1.3 percent, unspecified 6.2 percent (2011 estimate)

**RELIGION**
Protestant 32.1 percent, Roman Catholic 21.6 percent, Hindu 18.2 percent, Muslim 5 percent, Jehovah's Witness 1.5 percent, other 8.4 percent, none 2.2 percent, unspecified 11.1 percent (2011 estimate)

**LANGUAGES**
English (official), Trinidadian Creole English, Tobagonian Creole English, Trinidadian Hindustani, Trinidadian Creole French, Spanish, Chinese

**NATIONAL HOLIDAY**
Independence Day, August 31

# TIMELINE

| IN TRINIDAD AND TOBAGO | IN THE WORLD |
|---|---|
| **Before 300 BCE**<br>Hunter-gatherers live on the island of Trinidad. | |
| **300 BCE**<br>A second wave of settlers arrives on Tobago. | |
| **1000**<br>A group who can speak Carib dialects moves onto the islands. | **1206–1368**<br>Genghis Khan unifies the Mongols and starts their conquest of the world. At its height, the Mongol Empire under Kublai Khan stretches from China to Persia and parts of Europe and Russia. |
| **1498**<br>Christopher Columbus visits the islands. | |
| **1532**<br>Spain colonizes Trinidad, appointing a governor to rule it. | **1776**<br>The US Declaration of Independence is signed. |
| **1781**<br>The French capture Tobago from the Spanish, transforming it into a sugar-producing colony. | |
| **1797**<br>A British naval expedition captures Trinidad from Spain. | |
| **1802**<br>Spain cedes Trinidad to Great Britain under the Treaty of Amiens. | |
| **1814**<br>France cedes Tobago to Great Britain. | |
| **1834**<br>Slavery is abolished in the islands, though the slaves aren't fully freed until 1838. | **1837**<br>The reign of Queen Victoria begins in Britain. |
| **1845**<br>Indentured workers are brought in from India to work on sugar plantations. | |
| **1889**<br>Trinidad and Tobago are administratively combined as a single British colony. | **1914–1918**<br>World War I occurs.<br>**1939–1945**<br>World War II occurs. |
| **1959**<br>Trinidad and Tobago gains internal self-government, with Eric Williams as prime minister. | |
| **1962**<br>Trinidad and Tobago becomes independent. | |

| IN TRINIDAD AND TOBAGO | IN THE WORLD |
|---|---|
| **1976** Trinidad and Tobago becomes a republic. | |
| **1981** George Chambers becomes prime minister following Williams's death. | |
| **1986** Tobago-based National Alliance for Reconstruction (NAR) wins the general election. | **1986** A disaster at the Chernobyl nuclear power plant in Ukraine spreads radiation over a large area of the Soviet Union. |
| **1987** Noor Hassanali becomes president. | |
| **1991** Patrick Manning becomes prime minister. | |
| **1995** The Indian-based United National Congress (UNC) and NAR form coalition. | |
| **2002** The People's National Movement wins elections. | **2001** Terrorists attack the United States on September 11. |
| **2003** President George Maxwell Richards is sworn in. | **2003** The War in Iraq begins. |
| **2007** Plans are announced to end the centuries-old sugar industry. | **2009** Barack Obama becomes the US president. |
| **2010** Kamla Persad-Bissessar becomes the first female prime minister. | |
| **2015** Dr. Keith Christopher Rowley is sworn in as prime minister; the country enters a recession. | |
| **2016** Paula-Mae Weekes retires as judge on the nation's Court of Appeal. | **2016** Donald Trump is elected president of the United States. |
| **2018** Paula-Mae Weekes becomes the country's sixth president. | **2018** The United Nations Intergovernmental Panel on Climate Change warns that a "point of no return" could be reached in as little as 12 years. |
| **2019** Trinidad and Tobago's economy returns from recession. | **2020** US drones kill a top Iranian official; Iran fires missiles at a US air base in Iraq in response. |

# GLOSSARY

**callaloo**
A creole stew with the consistency of soup.

**climate change**
Change in Earth's weather caused by human activity.

**crest**
A fanlike feature on top of some birds' heads.

*dhalpuri* (dal-POUR-ee)
A type of roti bread that is made using two layers of dough to form a thin sandwich.

*dih* (DEE)
A spirit believed in by those who practice black magic.

**double entendre**
A word or phrase with two different meanings; one of the meanings is usually more suggestive.

**estuary**
An area where the ocean's tide meets a river.

**greenhouse gas**
A gas that comes from the burning of fossil fuels and harms the environment.

**gross domestic product (GDP)**
The total value of goods and services produced in a country in a year. GDP per capita is a measure that divides that total value by the country's population.

**imam**
A religious Islamic man who leads prayers in a mosque.

**midden**
A trash heap.

**muezzin**
A man who calls Muslims to prayer from a mosque minaret.

**obeah**
A traditional African form of witchcraft and medicine also practiced in the Caribbean.

*parang* (par-ANG)
Traditional Christmas music evolved from Spanish carols.

*parranderos* (par-an-DARE-owes)
The musicians who perform parang.

*pelau* (PEL-ow)
A creole dish of chicken, vegetables, and peas, featuring different spices.

*puja* (PU-ja)
A Hindu religious service.

**wattle**
The skin hanging from the neck of some birds, such as turkeys.

# FOR FURTHER INFORMATION

## BOOKS

Allen, Ray. *Jump Up!: Caribbean Carnival Music in New York City*. New York, NY: Oxford University Press, 2019.

Ganeshram, Ramin. *Sweet Hands: Island Cooking From Trinidad & Tobago*. New York, NY: Hippocrene Books, 2018.

Hernandez, Romel. *Trinidad and Tobago*. Philadelphia, PA: Mason Crest, 2016.

Parasram, Jai. *Beyond Survival: Indians in Trinidad and Tobago, 1845-2017*. Hertford, UK: Hansib Publications, 2018.

Pemberton, Rita, Debbie McCollin, Gelien Matthews, and Michael Toussaint. *Historical Dictionary of Trinidad and Tobago, New Edition*. Lanham, MD: Rowman & Littlefield, 2018.

Seepersad, Randy, and Dianne Williams. *Crime & Security in Trinidad and Tobago*. Kingston, Jamaica: Ian Randle Publishers, 2016.

## WEBSITES

CIA. *The World Factbook*. "Trinidad and Tobago." https://www.cia.gov/library/publications/the-world-factbook/geos/td.html.

The Official Trinidad and Tobago Travel and Tourism Site. http://www.gotrinidadandtobago.com.

Trinidad and Tobago Government Portal. http://www.ttconnect.gov.tt/gortt/portal/ttconnect.

US Department of State, Trinidad and Tobago. https://www.state.gov/u-s-relations-with-trinidad-and-tobago.

## FILMS

*NCBA/Samaroo's Kings & Queens of Trinidad & Tobago Carnival 2009*. Directed by R. Barry McComie. Advance Dynamics Ltd., 2009.

*Tacarigua: A Village in Trinidad and Tobago*. 2010.

## MUSIC

Calypso Rose. *Queen of Trinidad*. Maturity Music, 2012.

Machel Montano. *G.O.A.T.* Monk Music, 2019.

The Mighty Sparrow. *Fyaah and Fury*. BLS Records/VP Records, 2018.

# BIBLIOGRAPHY

Asa Wright Nature Centre. http://asawright.org.

CARICOM. https://caricom.org.

CIA. *The World Factbook*. "Trinidad and Tobago." https://www.cia.gov/library/publications/the-world-factbook/geos/td.html.

Destination Trinidad & Tobago. https://www.destinationtnt.com.

Environment Tobago. https://www.environmenttobago.net/node/1.

Ewbank, Tim. *Trinidad and Tobago*. London, UK: Kuperard, 2011.

Ganeshram, Ramin. *Sweet Hands: Island Cooking From Trinidad & Tobago*. New York, NY: Hippocrene Books, 2018.

Hernandez, Romel. *Trinidad and Tobago*. Philadelphia, PA: Mason Crest, 2016.

Jackson, Elijah. "Top 10 Facts About Living Conditions in Trinidad and Tobago," The Borgen Project. Accessed December 1, 2019. https://borgenproject.org/top-10-facts-about-living-conditions-in-trinidad-and-tobago.

Judiciary Trinidad and Tobago. http://www.ttlawcourts.org/index.php/about-the-judiciary-1/overview-53.

Lonely Planet. "Trinidad and Tobago." https://www.lonelyplanet.com/trinidad-and-tobago.

The Official Trinidad and Tobago Travel and Tourism Site. http://www.gotrinidadandtobago.com.

Pemberton, Rita, Debbie McCollin, Gelien Matthews, and Michael Toussaint. *Historical Dictionary of Trinidad and Tobago, New Edition*. Lanham, MD: Rowman & Littlefield, 2018.

Ramm, Benjamin. "The Subversive Power of Calypso Music." BBC.com, October 11, 2017. http://www.bbc.com/culture/story/20171010-the-surprising-politics-of-calypso.

Trinidad and Tobago Government Portal. http://www.ttconnect.gov.tt/gortt/portal/ttconnect.

Urosevich, Patti. *Trinidad and Tobago*. New York, NY: Chelsea House Publishers, 1988.

# INDEX

Africa/African, 5, 17, 25, 28, 31, 32, 37, 67, 68, 69, 73—74, 80, 84, 85, 87, 90, 93—94, 96, 101, 106, 112, 120, 125
agriculture, 7, 13, 21, 22—23, 25—26, 29, 48—51, 53, 55, 68, 69, 77, 128
animals, 11—16, 50, 51—52, 54, 61—65, 126
  bats, 13, 50, 63
  birds of paradise, 12, 17
  manatees, 15, 50, 61—62
  ocelots, 13
  oilbirds, 13
  scarlet ibis, 15, 50, 63
  sea turtles, 16, 50, 59, 62, 64
  Trinidad piping guan, 61
area, 9

beaches, 5, 15—16, 19, 50, 51, 59, 64, 111
Berrio, Antonio de, 22
Boldon, Ato, 114
Britain/British, 17, 22, 23—25, 26—31, 35—36, 37, 38, 40, 41, 46, 64, 68, 78, 84, 85, 106, 114, 120
Buccoo, 16, 19, 64

Calderón, Louisa, 24
Calypso Rose, 103, 104
Campbell, Shemika, 107
carbon emissions, 56—57, 59
CARICOM, 40, 46, 128
Cazabon, Michel-Jean, 109
Cedula of Population, 23, 67, 68
Chacón, José María, 14, 23
Chaguanas, 18, 122
China/Chinese, 17, 25, 69, 94, 123
climate, 10, 17, 119
climate change, 51, 55, 56, 59, 62
Columbus, Christopher, 21, 22, 67
Commonwealth of Nations, 31, 36, 114
conservation, 50, 55, 59—60, 63—65
constitution, 28, 30, 36, 83
coral reefs, 12, 16, 17, 19, 56, 64, 115
coup attempt, 32—33

court system, 38—40, 41
Crawford, Hasely, 114
crime, 40—41
crops
  cassava, 21, 69, 129
  cocoa, 22—23, 48, 49—51, 105
  cotton, 23, 25, 26
  sugar, 23, 25, 26, 29, 30, 45, 48, 49, 69, 96
currency, 15, 45, 48

dancing, 6, 85, 86, 101, 105, 112, 120, 121, 122
  limbo, 107
death penalty, 41
deforestation, 55, 63
drinks, 115, 127—128
  Angostura bitters, 75, 127

education, 30, 31, 36, 37, 59, 73, 74, 75, 78—79, 95, 96, 97
elections, 27, 28, 30, 31, 32, 36—38, 39, 43
emigration, 68

festivals
  Carnival, 6, 23, 71, 73, 77—78, 95, 102, 104, 105, 106, 109, 113, 116—117, 118, 119—121
  Dragon Boat Festival, 123
  fetes, 6, 71, 95, 99, 112, 117
  Santa Rosa Festival, 69
fishing, 19, 21, 51—52, 57, 62
flag, 37
food, 5, 7, 45, 49, 71, 74, 77, 87, 89, 97, 117, 125—127, 128, 129
  callaloo, 124, 126
  desserts, 128
  *pelau*, 97, 125—126, 130 (recipe)
  roti, 126—127
  *sawine*, 123
  seafood, 57, 124, 126, 129
food insecurity, 7, 128
foreign investment, 31, 45
forests, 5, 8, 12—13, 15—16, 21, 61, 64—65, 126

France/French, 17, 22, 23, 26, 29, 67, 68, 71, 94, 95—96, 119, 120

health, 7, 36, 57, 73, 79
highest point, 10
hills, 5, 8, 10, 11, 12, 13, 18, 19, 49, 50, 63, 75
Hislop, Thomas, 24
holidays
  Christmas, 71, 105—106, 120, 122
  Diwali, 71, 88, 122—123
  Eid al-Fitr, 89, 122, 123
  Hosay, 121—122
  Independence Day, 14, 122
  Shouter Baptist Liberation Day, 85—86, 122
housing, 36, 75—76, 77
hurricanes, 10, 12, 17, 26, 51, 64
indentured laborers, 25—26, 69, 87, 96, 106
independence, 30, 31, 35—36, 37
India/Indian, 17, 25—26, 31, 32, 37, 38, 42—43, 49, 67, 68—69, 74, 81, 83, 87—88, 89, 96—97, 101, 105, 106, 121, 126—127
indigenous groups, 17, 21, 22—23, 67, 93
  Arawaks, 21—22, 67
  Caribs, 18, 21—22, 67, 69

Jamaat al Muslimeen, 32—33

languages
  Chinese, 94
  Coco Payol, 97
  French, 23, 94, 95—96
  Hindi, 95, 96—97, 105
  Patois, 94
  pidgin, 93—94
  Spanish, 94, 96, 97, 105
  Standard English, 93, 94, 95, 96, 97
  Tobagonian Creole, 94
  Trinidadian Creole (Trini), 6, 93, 94, 95, 96, 97
Lebanon/Lebanese, 69

# INDEX

legislatures, 27, 31, 32, 33, 34, 35—38, 39, 96
liming, 95, 111—112, 114, 115
literature, 101, 106—108
Little Tobago, 12, 17, 65
Lord Shorty (Ras Shorty I), 105
Lovelace, Earl, 106

Manning, Patrick, 37, 38, 58
Maraj, Bhadase, 31, 42—43
markets, 7, 49, 76—77, 113—114, 129
marriage, 80—81, 88
media
  internet, 99
  newspapers, 28, 97—98
  radio, 99, 111, 112
  television, 98—99, 111
Mighty Sparrow, 104
missionaries, 22
museums, 18—19, 101, 108, 109
music
  calypso, 45, 71, 99, 102—105, 111, 112, 120—121
  chutney soca, 105
  parang, 105—106
  reggae, 99, 112
  soca, 99, 102, 103—105, 115
  steel bands, 45, 100, 101—102, 120

Naipaul, V. S., 106—108
natural gas, 6, 45, 46, 47, 49, 53, 56, 128
nature reserves, 13, 15, 63—65, 126
nightclubs, 113

obeah, 90—91
oil, 6, 18, 27, 29, 31, 37, 44, 45, 46—47, 48, 53, 56, 57, 58, 75, 113, 128

Panday, Basdeo, 38, 43
Paria, Gulf of, 9, 17, 18, 30, 56, 57
Persad-Bissessar, Kamla, 35, 38, 39, 43
petrochemical industry, 6, 45, 48, 57
Picton, Thomas, 23—24
Pitch Lake, 11, 27, 47, 90

plant life, 11—12, 13, 14, 60, 61, 62, 63
  chaconia (wild poinsettia), 14
  mangroves, 11, 12, 14, 15, 56, 63
  sundew, 13
Pointe-à-Pierre, 18, 46, 63—64
Point Lisas, 18, 48
political parties
  National Alliance for Reconstruction (NAR), 32, 37—38, 43
  People's Democratic Party (PDP), 31, 37, 42, 43
  People's National Movement (PNM), 30, 31, 32, 33, 36, 37—38, 39
  People's Partnership, 38
  United National Congress (UNC), 33, 38, 39, 43
pollution, 55, 56—57, 62, 77
population, 17, 18, 23, 26, 46, 48, 55, 60, 67, 68—69, 75, 77, 78, 79, 83—84, 99
Port of Spain, 5, 7, 13, 17—18, 23, 24, 26, 27, 31, 33, 39, 40, 42, 51, 58, 68, 69, 70, 75, 76, 78, 79, 80, 82, 84, 89, 100, 108, 114, 115, 116—117, 129
poverty, 25, 26, 29, 46, 77, 79

racism, 28, 73, 102, 106
recession, 6, 52—53
recycling, 59—60
refugees, 70, 97
religions
  Christian, 22, 67, 69, 71, 73, 78, 82, 83, 84, 85, 87, 90, 117, 120
  Hindu, 42, 69, 71, 81, 83, 84, 87—88, 119, 122—123
  Muslim, 32, 42, 69, 83, 87, 88—89, 119, 121—122, 123
  Orisha, 84, 85, 86
  Rastafarian, 72, 73, 84, 87
  Shouter (Spiritual) Baptist, 83, 84, 85—86
riots, 26—27, 29, 33, 120
rivers, 10—11, 12, 14, 56, 61
Robinson, A. N. R., 32, 37, 38, 43
Roffey, Monique, 108

Rowley, Keith Christopher, 32, 33, 38, 39, 45, 46, 70, 78, 128

San Fernando, 5, 18, 40, 58, 75, 76, 114, 121
Scarborough, 5, 18—19, 51, 72, 76, 78, 80, 110
Selvon, Samuel, 106
slavery, 22, 23, 24—26, 68, 69, 73, 85, 90, 91, 93—94, 96, 102, 120
Smyth, Amanda, 108
Spain/Spanish, 14, 17, 22, 23, 24, 26, 67, 68, 97, 105
Speyside, 12, 64, 65
spirits, 85, 86, 89—90, 95
sports, 105, 111, 114—116
strikes, 28, 29, 31
swamps, 10, 15, 50, 63

terrorism, 42
tourism, 5, 6, 11, 16, 18, 19, 45, 50, 51, 56, 59, 63, 70, 77, 93, 113
trade, 7, 17—18, 48, 49, 51, 52, 75, 77, 127, 128
transportation
  airports, 18, 19, 51, 79, 80
  buses, 79—80
  ferries, 80
  roads, 58, 77
  water taxis, 58

United States, 25, 27, 29—30, 31, 49, 57, 74, 76, 77, 78, 85, 98—99, 105, 107, 113

Venezuela, 5, 9, 10, 11, 17, 21, 57, 67, 70, 77, 97, 105, 127
voting rights, 30, 35

Walcott, Derek, 106
waste management, 59—60
water supply, 26, 60, 75
Weekes, Paula-Mae, 36, 39
Williams, Eric, 30, 31, 32, 42
World War I, 28
World War II, 29—30, 102, 106, 120